Barnsley Librar

CLASSIFICATION
AND INDEXING
PRACTICE

CLASSIFICATION AND INDEXING PRACTICE

K G B Bakewell

MA FLA AMBIM

Senior Lecturer
Department of Library and Information Studies
Liverpool Polytechnic

CLIVE BINGLEY
LONDON

LINNET BOOKS
HAMDEN · CONN

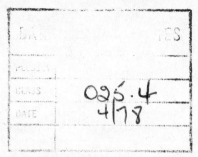
FIRST PUBLISHED 1978 BY CLIVE BINGLEY LTD
16 PEMBRIDGE ROAD LONDON W11 UK
SIMULTANEOUSLY PUBLISHED IN THE USA BY LINNET BOOKS
A DIVISION OF THE SHOE STRING PRESS INC
995 SHERMAN AVENUE HAMDEN CONNECTICUT 06514
SET IN 10 ON 11 POINT THEME BY ALLSET
PRINTED AND BOUND IN THE UK BY
REDWOOD BURN LTD TROWBRIDGE AND ESHER
COPYRIGHT © K G B BAKEWELL 1978
ALL RIGHTS RESERVED
BINGLEY ISBN: 0 85157 247 2
LINNET ISBN: 0 208 01671 6

Library of Congress Cataloging in Publication Data

Bakewell, K G B
    Classification and indexing practice.

    Bibliography: p.
    Includes index.
    1. Classification—Books.   2. Indexing   I. Title.
Z696.A4B34   025.4   77-16467
ISBN 0-208-01671-6

CONTENTS

FIGURES

PREFACE

THERE ARE several textbooks which provide good descriptions of the principles behind classification and indexing systems. There are one or two reports which summarize the classification and indexing practices of a number of libraries: some, such as the survey by Comaromi and associates on the use of the Dewey Decimal Classification and the Institute on the Library of Congress Classification, are mentioned in succeeding chapters; others include Keith Davison's *Classification practice in Britain* (London, Library Association, 1966) and the report by Joan Friedman and Alan E Jeffreys *Cataloguing and classification in British university libraries* (Sheffield, University of Sheffield Postgraduate School of Librarianship, 1967). I think, however, that this is the first attempt to take a number of libraries and examine in some detail how they use particular classification and/or indexing systems. That is my apologia for this book, which I hope will be useful to the practitioner and student.

Some prior knowledge of classification and indexing systems is assumed, and in particular I would hope that my readers are familiar with the books by Foskett and Maltby in the basic reading list (page 196). I certainly do not regard this book as a rival to these three works, and I have tried to avoid repeating information which can easily be found in them. For this reason my descriptions of systems have been kept to an absolute minimum and I have concentrated on the practical experiences of my case studies. (There is, in any case, a danger for the student in providing too much descriptive information about classification schemes, since it may encourage him not to examine the schemes themselves—a frequent complaint of examiners.)

Similarly, I have in general avoided giving my own views about particular systems, preferring to concentrate on the opinions of the practitioners with whom I have spoken.

The book is about classification and indexing *practice*, and for this reason I have avoided reference to experimental systems which at present have few practical applications. I have also ignored non-current schemes like Cutter's Expansive Classification even though Robert L

Mowery ('The Cutter Classification: still at work' *Library resources and technical services* 20(2) spring 1976, 154-156) has identified twelve US and Canadian libraries still using it. In 1977 one cannot take too seriously a scheme which has not been revised since 1891, although it has had a strong influence on other schemes such as the Library of Congress Classification.

Unless otherwise stated, my descriptions have been derived from visits to libraries, and it follows that the book could not have been written without the generous co-operation of colleagues in the following organizations who gave up their time to talk to me and checked what I had to say about their libraries' practices. Bedford College (University of London); Birmingham Public Libraries; Birmingham School of Music (now part of the City of Birmingham Polytechnic); the British Institute of Management; the British Library (Library Association Library); the British Library (Science Reference Library); the British Standards Institution Technical Help for Exporters; Cheltenham Ladies' College; the City of London Polytechnic; The City University, London; Codsall High School; Croham Hurst School, South Croydon; the Department of Health and Social Security; the Departments of the Environment and Transport; Edinburgh City Libraries; Hazel Grove High School, Stockport; ICI Fibres, Harrogate; the Inner London Education Authority Central Library Resources Service; the Inner London Education Authority School Library Service; the Institute of Practitioners in Work Study, Organisation and Methods; Metal Box Limited; the National Foundation for Educational Research in England and Wales; the National Library of Scotland; Parliament Hill School, London; St Thomas the Apostle School, Peckham, London; the Schools Council; Sheffield City Polytechnic; South Trafford College of Further Education, Altrincham; the Tavistock Joint Library; the University of Bath; the University of Bradford; the University of Lancaster; the University of Liverpool; the University of London Institute of Education; the Wessex Medical Library, University of Southampton; Wigan Reference Library; and the Zoological Society of London. I am most grateful to them as well as to colleagues at Liverpool Polytechnic and to E T (Bill) Bryant, J C Downing and R R Trotter for reading sections of the manuscript and saving me from a number of errors.

If this book is a success it will be due in no small measure to help given willingly by colleagues. If it is a failure the fault will be entirely mine.

K G B BAKEWELL

Liverpool
July 1977

10

ABBREVIATIONS AND ACRONYMS USED

AACR	Anglo-American Cataloguing Rules
BC	Bliss's Bibliographic Classification
BCM	British Catalogue of Music (classification)
BIM	British Institute of Management
BLAISE	British Library Automated Information Service
BLCMP	Birmingham Libraries Co-operative Mechanisation Project
BNB	British National Bibliography
BSD	Bibliographic Services Division (of the British Library)
BTI	British Technology Index
CC	Colon Classification
CLW	College of Librarianship Wales
CRG	Classification Research Group (classification of library and information science)
DC	Dewey Decimal Classification
DHSS	Department of Health and Social Security
ERIC	Educational Resources Information Center
FID	International Federation for Documentation
ILEA	Inner London Education Authority
KWIC	Keyword-in-context
KWOC	Keyword-out-of-context
LA	Library Association
LC	Library of Congress (classification)
LCBS	London Classification of Business Studies
LCSH	Library of Congress Subject Headings
LEC	London Education Classification
LISA	Library and Information Science Abstracts
MARC	Machine readable cataloguing
MEDLARS	Medical Literature Analysis and Retrieval System
MEDLINE	MEDLARS on-line
MERLIN	Machine readable library information
MeSH	Medical subject headings
NBM	Non-book materials
NFER	National Foundation for Educational Research in England and Wales

NLM	National Library of Medicine (classification)
NUC	National Union Catalog
OCCI	Optical Coincidence Co-ordinate Indexing
OSTI	Office for Scientific and Technical Information
PMEST	Personality, matter, energy, space, time
PRECIS	Preserved Context Index System
SLIC	Selective Listing in Combination
SRL	British Library (Science Reference Library)
THE	Technical Help for Exporters (British Standards Institution)
UDC	Universal Decimal Classification
WML	Wessex Medical Library

Chapter one

THE DEWEY DECIMAL CLASSIFICATION

MELVIL DEWEY's Decimal Classification (DC), the first edition of which appeared in 1876, remains the most widely used library classification in the world and has been aptly described by Joel Downing as 'the classification upon which the sun never sets.'[1] A true pioneer in the field, Dewey introduced *relative location*, made possible by a *decimal notation*, although some have criticized the arbitrary division into ten main classes, further divided into ten subclasses, etc, which this decimal notation produced. Another major innovation was the *relative index*, an insurance against 'losing' material (ie scattering aspects of a topic) in the classified sequence.

There have now been eighteen editions of the full schedules, the eighteenth having been published in 1971, and work is proceeding actively on the nineteenth edition. There have also been ten abridged editions since 1894, the tenth having been published in 1971.

One reason for the popularity of DC in the English-speaking world is the inclusion of DC numbers on the printed catalogue cards, MARC tapes and bibliographies/catalogues issued by the Library of Congress and the British Library Bibliographic Services Division, publishers of the *British national bibliography*. Between them, according to Melba Davis Adams,[2] these two organizations apply DC numbers to ninety per cent of books published in the English language throughout the world. Joyce Bruin has outlined some of the problems encountered by BNB in attempting to achieve uniformity with the Decimal Classification Division of the Library of Congress in the application of DC numbers.[3] Increased co-operation between the two organizations has gone some way towards solving these problems, as demonstrated by the views of two exchangees, Melba Davis Adams and Robert Ross Trotter,[4] who each spent six weeks with the foreign organization.

Dewey in the United States and Canada

John P Comaromi, Mary Ellen Michael and Janet Bloom have shown that, in spite of the much publicized trend away from DC to the Library of Congress Classification (see chapter three), DC continues to enjoy wide popularity in the United States and Canada.[5] For their survey, conducted in 1975 for Forest Press (publishers of DC), they sent questionnaires to ten per cent of public libraries, ten per cent of junior college libraries and ten per cent of university libraries listed in *American library directory 1974-75*. They also included all academic and public libraries containing 500,000 volumes or more, whether or not they were in the original sample, and all known commercial processing centres (totalling ninety-three).

They found that 85.4 per cent of the total sample (representing 658 libraries in the US and 121 in Canada) were using DC but only 37.7 per cent of US libraries containing 500,000 volumes or more and 27.8 per cent of Canadian libraries containing an equal number of volumes.

This report provides a wealth of detail concerning the application of DC in North America. The following are just a few of the facts and opinions recorded:

1 The vast majority of DC users in the sample (516) used the eighteenth full edition as their primary edition, followed by sixty-one using the seventeenth, thirty-seven using the sixteenth, seven using the fifteenth, five using the fourteenth and five using an earlier edition. The tenth abridged edition was used by 125 libraries, the ninth by fifty-four libraries, the eighth by twenty-six libraries and an earlier abridged edition by three libraries. It is surprising that 160 public libraries quoted an abridged edition as their primary edition, three of them using an earlier abridgment than the eighth.

2 Nearly half the DC users in the sample imposed a limit on the number of digits after the decimal point. In the case of more than half of these, this limit was three digits but 8.6 per cent made it six digits or more.

3 Only 26.1 per cent of DC users adopted the DC preferred method of classifying biographies under subject. Yet 56.5 per cent thought DC should *continue* to classify biography with subject as the preferred method. This indicates a certain inconsistency in those answering the questionnaires.

4 More than half the sample made changes as announced in *Decimal classification additions, notes and decisions (DC&)*. This indicates that, contrary to popular belief, people do read interim bulletins.

5 The use of 04 as a symbol to introduce 'general special' topics was criticized by a number of British library school lecturers when it was introduced into the eighteenth edition, because of the illogical arrangement it caused by splitting general form divisions as in the following example:

332   Financial economics
332.03   Encyclopedias of financial economics
332.04   'general special'

332.041	Capital
332.05	Periodicals on financial economics.

Asked whether they objected to the placement of 04 between dictionaries and serials, 10.6 per cent said yes, 30.2 per cent said no and 59.3 per cent had no opinion. This could indicate that librarians are not worried by illogical order or perhaps that library school lecturers are obsessed with academic considerations.

6 Asked whether classifiers found the index to the eighteenth edition satisfactory, nearly eighty per cent said yes or sometimes. Surprisingly, only 8.8 per cent did not like this much-criticized feature of the eighteenth edition. 11.6 per cent had no opinion about the index, which is perhaps even more staggering!

7 589 libraries (69.5 per cent of the DC users in the sample) said that they would not consider changing from DC to the Library of Congress Classification. The other libraries might change if staff were available (11.2 per cent), if DC numbers switched back and forth from edition to edition (8.4 per cent), if the network began to use another classification (8.3 per cent), if DC revisions became too drastic (7.9 per cent) or too frequent (6.4 per cent), if LC became more economical (6.8 per cent), if DC became out-of-date (five per cent) or if DC became inadequate for specialized collections (4.1 per cent).

The overall picture in this important report is of a classification scheme which is thriving but which certainly does not please all librarians all of the time.

Dewey in Britain

In July 1972 the Library Association's Research Department sent questionnaires, at the request of the Dewey Decimal Classification Subcommittee of the Library Association, to 1016 libraries in Great Britain. Of the 940 libraries which returned completed questionnaires, 744 used DC for their main collection of books (441 public libraries, 265 college libraries, twenty-seven university libraries and eleven others).[6] The editions in use varied considerably, the most popular being the sixteenth (1958), used by 181 libraries, and the eighteenth (1971), used by 152 libraries. Staggeringly, one library was using the fifth edition (1894) and one was using the eleventh (1922). Eight libraries were using the thirteenth edition (1952), alone or supplemented by later editions, and 106 were using the fourteenth edition (1942), alone or supplemented by later editions. 203 libraries were considering changing to the eighteenth full edition or the tenth abridged edition during the following two years.

The survey showed that DC was used in 441 out of 447 public libraries (98.6 per cent). Following local government reorganization in 1974, this figure must be very nearly one hundred per cent though at least one public library (Edinburgh) prefers the Library of Congress Classification (see pages 61-64).

The British Library's Working Party on Classification and Indexing found that in 1973 DC was being used by approximately forty-seven per cent of all libraries in Britain and that approximately seventy-five per cent of the total library holdings in Britain were being classified by DC.[7]

Many public libraries use BNB printed cards or subscribe to the UK MARC service, but this does not necessarily mean that they accept without question the DC class numbers provided by the *British national bibliography*. Even if they do, they often make adjustments in their shelf arrangement such as separating books about music from music scores, collocating language and literature and/or history and travel (for example German history at 943, German travel at T43 or 943T), and ignoring the preferred method of classifying biography (scattering by subject) in favour of collecting biography alphabetically or systematically at 920 or B. Fiction is, of course, normally arranged alphabetically by author.

Liverpool City Libraries provides an example of a large central library system which, although generally accepting DC numbers as given in BNB, makes considerable adjustments in its shelf arrangement to meet the needs of subject departmentalization. For example the International Library collects language, literature, archaeology, travel and history, so that Italian language, literature, archaeology, travel and history are shelved together although classified at 450, 850, 913.45, 914.5 and 945. The Commercial and Social Sciences Library consists of three distinct sections: the Commercial Library proper, taking 330 (Economics), 380 (Commerce) and 650 (Management); the Social Sciences Library, taking 300 (Social Sciences in general), 310 (Statistics), 360 (Social Welfare), 370 (Education) and 390 (Customs, apart from 391, Costume, which is in the Art Library); and the Law Library, taking 320 (Politics), 340 (Law) and 350 (Administration). The need to make these adjustments clearly indicates some of the problems of DC, in spite of improvements made in successive editions. It also shows how broken order can be used effectively, provided there is adequate guiding.

Some of the experiences of eleven British non-public libraries in the use of DC are described below.

University of Bradford
The University of Bradford decided to adopt DC for sections of its stock when it achieved university status in 1966. Previously, as a College of Advanced Technology, it had used UDC, but this was

16

considered unsuitable for subjects outside the areas of science and technology. When the academic staff were shown sections of DC for social sciences and related subjects (including psychology), they agreed that it was superior to UDC for their requirements. (This was the seventeenth edition of DC, which was the edition in which the curious separation of aspects of psychology at 130 and 150 was corrected.)

The university preferred to retain UDC for science and technology, which in any case it would have been impractical to reclassify, as a result of which there are two classification schemes in use in the library: UDC for science and technology and DC for all other subjects. This might be considered difficult for staff and users but in fact it presented few problems, mainly because of the initial breakdown of all the stock into twenty-three broad subject areas, each represented by a letter of the alphabet, thus:

A General works
B Philosophy; Religion
C Geography; History; Archaeology
D Psychology; Social sciences; Social services; Demography; Politics; Law; Government; Education
E Economics; Commerce; Business organization and management
F Languages; Literature
G Fine arts; Photography; Music; Theatre; Sport
H History of science and technology
L Mathematics (including statistics and computers)
M Physics
N Chemistry; Crystallography; Mineralogy
P Astronomy; Geology; Geomorphology
Q Palaeontology; Anthropology; General biology
R Botany; Agriculture
S Zoology; Medicine (including pharmacy and opthalmic optics)
T Applied science and engineering in general; Patents and inventions; Materials and materials testing
U Control, mechanical, transport engineering
V Nuclear engineering
W Electrical and electronic engineering
X Surveying; Civil engineering; Building; Town and country planning; Architecture
Y Chemical technology; Chemical engineering; Manufacturing trades (including dyeing, metallurgy, textiles, plastics, printing)
Z Bibliographies; Encyclopedias

The appropriate DC or UDC class number follows this initial letter:

D300   Social sciences
D301   Sociology
D301.1   Social psychology
D301.15   Group behaviour

17

The use of DC for a large part of the stock has advantages from the point of view of using centralized services, but the university does not find it possible to accept all class numbers allotted by BSD. There are two reasons for this. Firstly, over the years there have been extensive amendments made to the seventeenth (and later the eighteenth) editions of DC to meet the special needs of the university; and, secondly, like so many libraries, it cannot guarantee to accept each edition of DC without amendment, as BSD has committed itself to doing, since this could involve wholesale reclassification.

The major amendment made by the library is the classification of social welfare at 306 instead of 360 in order to collocate it with the social sciences in general. Like many libraries, the university ignores, for individual writers, a) the distinction between American and English literature, using 810 only for works about American literature in general, and b) the chronological divisions provided at 821-829. All English and American poets are arranged alphabetically at 821, dramatists alphabetically at 822 etc. This is another decision which meets with the strong approval of the academic staff. (The well-known problem in DC of the separation of language and literature is solved at Bradford by the use of the initial letter F for languages and literature.)

Other amendments are made to cater for British rather than American needs, such as

329	Political parties
329.1	Conservative party
329.2	Liberal Party
329.3	Labour Party
329.4	Independent Labour Party

or to provide for greater detail than is provided in the schedules, such as

	Bradford usage	DC18
150	Psychology	as Bradford
152	Physiological and experimental psychology	as Bradford
152.4	Emotions and feelings	as Bradford
152.43	Types of emotions	as Bradford
152.432	Primitive and uncontrolled emotions	as Bradford
152.4321	Love	—
152.4322	Envy. Hate	—
152.4323	Ecstasy. Elation	—
152.4324	Fear	—
152.4325	Anxiety	—
152.4326	Grief	—
152.4327	Shame. Guilt	—

There is occasional provision for 'facet analysis' where DC has ignored the possibilities, as at 301.1 Social psychology where the subdivisions enumerated at 301.112/.114 are replaced by the instruction 'divide as 150' so that 301.1124322 is used for hostility in the area of social psychology, adding the '24322' following 15 to 301.11.

Non-book materials are classified by DC or UDC in exactly the same way as books, and complete integration is practised both on the shelves and in the catalogue. In addition to the main subject entry in the classified catalogue, each form of material is given an additional entry under the UDC class number representing its form (see page 48).

Bedford College (University of London)

When it was decided to reclassify the library of Bedford College in 1969, DC was preferred to other possible contenders—the Library of Congress, Bliss's Bibliographic Classification and the Universal Decimal Classification—largely because it came nearest to satisfying the five features suggested by the librarian in his report to the Library Committee as being desirable in the new classification. a) It is reasonably up-to-date; b) apart from the separation of language and literature, its order of main subjects is acceptable; c) its notation displays order clearly and is practical, memorable, easily expansible and adaptable; d) it has a useful relative index; e) it is familiar to library staff and, through their use of public libraries, to users.

Apart from these points in its favour, the use of DC in the *British national bibliography* was considered a powerful argument for adopting the scheme. Even though the library did not use BNB cards, nor, at that time, did it contemplate using MARC tapes, the facility for checking classification in BNB was considered a major advantage.

The change to DC was welcomed by the library staff, who were familiar with the scheme and appreciated the much simpler notation than that of the superseded home-made scheme as indicated by the following comparative examples:

	Previous scheme	DC
British union catalogue of periodicals	LX.6414	016.05
Encyclopedia Britannica	L1.116	032
Saint-Exupéry, A de *Lettre à un ôtage*	H42.8786502	848*
Saint-Exupéry, A de *Terre des hommes*	H42.8786503	848*
		(*amended class number)

Reactions from students were also favourable, though some members of the academic staff were less happy and displayed that well-known phenomenon, 'resistance to change'. Sociologists generally favoured the reclassification but disliked the separation of social science topics within class 300 as shown by the following examples from Bedford College's chain index:

Poor: social conditions	301.4494
Poor *see also* Poverty	

Poverty: children: social welfare	362.785
Poverty: local government	352.9445
Poverty: macroeconomics	339.46
Poverty: social classes: sociology	301.4494
Poverty: social law	344.0325
Poverty: social welfare	362.5
Poverty: social welfare: central government administration	350.845
Poverty: United States: public administration	353.93845

A further disadvantage for academic staff is the scattering of 'disciplines' like Classics (appearing in 100, 870, 880 and 930) and Geography (in 330, 380, 550 and 910). A partial solution to this problem of geography is the provision of a separate 'area' catalogue listing all material relating to a country, with its own subject index. For example in the area subject index one finds

United States   A73

at A73 there are cards for every book in the library on the United States, arranged in DC order, such as

A73
shelved at   370.973 BOW

BOWLE, Samuel and GINTIS, Herbert
Schooling in capitalist America; educational reform and the contradictions of economic life. Routledge & KP, 1976.

Several changes were made to the DC schedules in order to present a more satisfactory sequence for the library. For example 150 (Psychology) includes all the material from 130 (which is deleted) and also incorporates psycho-linguistics from 400; 301 (Sociology) includes Customs at 301.6 (classified in DC at 390); and 338 (Industrial economics) includes Management at 338.75, divided like 658 (eg Personnel management at 338.753 instead of 658.3). Class 100 (Philosophy) is completely restructured, a major innovation being the collection at 190 of all works by and about major modern philosophers irrespective of the nationality or the philosopher or the subject matter of the individual work. For example, all works by Kant are classified at 190 KAN and are immediately followed on the shelves (and in the catalogue) by works about Kant arranged by the initial letter of the commentator, eg 190 KAN/A, 190 KAN/B.

Class 510 (Mathematics) has also been completely restructured, as seen in the following example:

	Bedford College	DC
511	Mathematical logic and foundations of mathematics	Mathematics — generalities
511.11	Elementary and introductory books	—
511.12	Philosophy and foundations of mathematics	—
511.13	Sources and classical works	—
511.14	Collections etc	—
511.2	Mathematical logic and metamathematics	Inductive and intuitive mathematics
511.3	Model theory and its applications	Symbolic (mathematical logic)
511.4	Intuitionism and constructivity	Approximations and expansions
511.5	Recursion theory	Theory and construction graphs
511.6	Automata and languages	Combinatorial analysis

In Class 800 (Literature), primary division is by period, thus:

	Bedford College	DC
820	English literature	English literature
821	Old English literature	English poetry
822	Middle English literature (1050-1500)	English drama
823	16th century English literature	English fiction
824	Shakespeare	English essays
825	17th century English literature	English speeches
826	18th century English literature	English letters
827	19th century English literature	English satire and humour
828	20th century English literature	English miscellaneous writings

Periods are subdivided by form where appropriate:

827	19th Century English literature
827.1	Poetry
827.2	Drama

As with individual philosophers, works by an individual writer are collected at the period number and are followed on the shelves and in

21

the catalogue by works about that writer. For example, all works on Milton are classified at 825 MIL followed immediately by works about him.

Although the library staff are aware of the disadvantages of making large scale amendments to the published schedules, they feel it is important to make adjustments to the classification if by so doing it becomes more acceptable to the academic staff. The philosophy and mathematics schedules were drafted by those departments and the English department welcomed the primary division by period as a more helpful arrangement reflecting the nature of their teaching.

The City University, London
The City University began reclassifying its library from UDC to DC in 1970 for several reasons. a) DC's notation is simpler; b) it is more up-to-date; c) it is easier to learn; d) DC numbers are available from centralized agencies in Britain and the United States and e) UDC attempts unsuccessfully to cater for shelf location and information retrieval. It was decided more appropriate to allow the classification scheme to cater for location only (which DC does more satisfactorily than UDC because of its simpler location), using the catalogue for information retrieval. However, as Peter Butcher (Head of Bibliographical Services) readily admits, the failure to provide a good subject catalogue has led to very inadequate subject access. He feels, though, that his point remains valid, and that the situation would be worse if compounded by the complex and often inscrutable shelf-mark notation of UDC.

A positive result of the change, from the point of view of economy, is that approximately 15,000 books (representing some 11,000 titles) were given DC class numbers by one person (occupying half his total time at work) during 1974/75 as compared with approximately 4,000 titles classified by UDC in 1970/71.

There has been little reaction to enable an assessment of the success or otherwise of this reclassification exercise from the point of view of the user except that the changes in the organization of mathematics were warmly welcomed.

Although availability of class numbers on centralized services was one reason for the change, class marks provided on MARC tapes or in the BNB are not used without question for a number of reasons— notably delay in recording material in centralized services and the need to gear classification to the requirements of the institution. However there is agreement with BNB or LC classing in eighty per cent of cases where they provide a DC class number. It is likely that the DC numbers on UK MARC retrospective files will be used to enable the speedy reclassification of pre-1971 items.

There are several deviations from 'standard' DC including the abolition of 690 (Building) and the classification of all material on building at 624 (Civil engineering); the classification of Social services at 301.17 instead of 360; and the use of completely redrafted schedules for 020 (Library and information science) and 532 (Fluid mechanics), examples from which are given below:

	City University	DC
025.3	Documentation. Information retrieval	Cataloguing
025.32	Cataloguing	Descriptive cataloguing
025.33	Descriptive cataloguing	Subject cataloguing
025.4	Classification and subject cataloguing	Classification
025.47	Subject indexing (029.5 in DC)	—
025.48	Abstracting (029.4 in DC)	—
532	Mechanics of fluids	Mechanics of fluids
532.1	Mechanics of liquids	Mechanics of liquids
532.2	Mechanics of gases (533 in DC)	Hydrostatics
532.3	Statics of fluids	—
532.4	Mass, density, specific gravity of fluids	Mass, density, specific gravity of liquids
532.5	Dynamics of fluids	Hydrodynamics (kinetics and kinematics of liquids)
532.501	Dynamics of liquids	—
532.502	Dynamics of gases	—
532.503	Dynamics of colloids, of fluid-particle systems	—
532.5031	Aerosols	—
532.5032	Sediment transport	—
532.504	Dynamics of plasma	—
532.5041	Magnetohydrodynamics	—
532.5042	Radioactive fluid mechanics	—

Analytical chemistry (543) is also completely restructured to give a more acceptable sequence, with all subdivisions at 543 and DC notations 544 and 545 unused.

The revised area table numbers for Great Britain are applied, except that 41 is used for the European Economic Community instead of Great Britain, which remains at 42.

The City University library classifies its non-book materials by DC in the same way as its bookstock, integration being practised in the catalogue but not on the shelves. A separate media catalogue is provided as a selective listing of the library's catalogue which has, since early 1976, been produced by the British Library Local Cataloguing Service (LOCAS).

City of London Polytechnic

The City of London Polytechnic was formed in 1970 by the amalgamation of a number of colleges which between them used several different classification schemes—the Bliss Bibliographic Classification, UDC, various editions of DC, and home-made classification schemes. It was decided that the library and learning resources service should use the DC18 for a number of reasons, most notably the fact that it would allow the use of the UK MARC services with a minimum of amendment. Other attractive features of DC were familiarity to users and frequency of revision, meaning that it would always be reasonably up-to-date. This contrasted strongly with the two most viable alternatives, Bliss and UDC: although a revision of Bliss was in sight, it was not considered practicable to wait for it, and there was a question mark over the future of UDC.

The only major amendment to 'official' DC is the use of 342-348 to represent British law without the use of 41 from the area tables, all foreign law being classified at 349. Variation of classification to meet the needs of particular courses is not considered desirable, especially as so many courses are of an interdisciplinary nature: the consistent application of an objective principle is much preferred to 'classification by purpose'. Only rarely, therefore, except in the case of class 340, will the City of London Polytechnic deviate from a MARC class number.

DC is used for non-book materials in exactly the same way as for books. There is an integrated classified catalogue, supported by a PRECIS subject index (see pages 157-8). There is also a separate non-print resources catalogue, produced partly to encourage the use of these resources (see figure one).

South Trafford College of Further Education

At South Trafford College of Further Education the sixteenth edition of DC is used in a simplified form. A major amendment is that everything relating to environmental problems (such as water and air pollution) is classified at 574.5, other DC numbers like 614.7 and

001.43307
A tape-slide guide on report literature — Leeds Polytechnic and British Library Lending Division. (s.l.): Leeds Polytechnic, 1974.
SOUND TAPE cassette. 2 tracks, mono. 1 cassette, 25 mins.
SLIDE SET. 5x5cm. 56 slide col.
(Tape slides in librarianship, no. IS/1).
On spine: Report literature.
CA777350ref

x1338

001.64
SHELVED AT 621.38195
Computers for the layman.

001.64
Hardware in action. London: BBC, for the Open University, 1976.
VIDEOTAPE cassette. Philip VCR, 625 lines, 50Hz, 1/2 in., b & w. 1 cassette, 25 minssound.
(An algorithmic approach to computing). (M251).
Contents: Builds up a diagram of a computer which shows the functions of the computers five main components and their interrelations.
BS776152

x1149

016.37
NICEM indexes on microfiche — NICEM
1974-75. Los Angeles (Calif.): University of Southern California, (1970-1976).
MICROFICHE. 10 1/2 x 15cm. 69 fiches b & w.

Contents: Index to Educational Audio Tapes (1st. ed)
Index to Educational Slides (2nd. ed)   Index to Educational Overhead Transparencies (4th. ed) Index to 35mm Educational Filmstrips (5th. ed) Update of Non Book Media Index to Psychology — Multimedia (2nd. ed)   Index to Producers and Distributors (3rd. ed). 773100 held by Media Librarian.
CA773100

x1287

Figure 1: Extract from the City of London Polytechnic's classified catalogue of non-print resources

628.5 being ignored. Map reading is placed at 912.01 instead of 526 to allow collocation with maps, thus anticipating DC18 which uses 912.014. As at the University of Bradford, British political parties are enumerated instead of American ones at 329.

Problems faced include having to deal with multi-faceted topics such as the sociology of developing countries and with new courses such as social biology, which includes elements of biology, health, medicine and other subjects. The library is considering changing to DC18 but reclassification presents problems in a very busy library with only a small staff.

Non-book materials are not classified but arranged numerically within forms of material (eg charts, cassettes, records). An integrated alphabetical subject index enables users to see at a glance what books and other materials are available on any subject and also allows indexing under as many terms as is considered practical when an item may be approached from several angles (see pages 145-7).

ILEA Central Library Resources Service

The Inner London Education Authority's Media Resources Centre was opened in 1971, its purposes being to support and encourage the use of learning resources in the authority's schools and colleges. The development of the centre's library and information service, which provides a large reference collection of audio-visual materials, has been described by Shifrin.[8]

During 1977 the ILEA started to reorganize its library resources services. The MRC library has moved to Vauxhall where it is in the process of being integrated with a collection of 20,000 books to form the reference library and information service at the ILEA's new Centre for Learning Resources. However its classification practice remains as described, since the MRC library was always seen by its librarian as part of a potential integrated service.

Shifrin states that 'at the MRC library, we have always felt that the division between books and other material is indefensible', so it is not surprising that the most popular book classification—DC18—should have been chosen to classify the library. This scheme was chosen because all but four of the 1200 schools associated with the centre were using an edition of DC. (Three of the remaining four were using the Bliss Bibliographic Classification and the other was using the Cheltenham Classification.)

The centre was not influenced in 1971 by BNB's use of DC but that would certainly be an influencing factor now, since BNB class numbers are used for those materials which are listed in BNB.

The centre makes very few amendments to DC18 except that it does not apply those form divisions concerned with physical forms of material because arrangement on the shelves is by physical form of material, as follows:

Small book-like materials (ie materials which are self-supporting on the shelves such as cassettes and film-loops)

Large book-like materials

Postcards

Filmstrips

Slides

Discs

Wallcharts

Portfolios

Packs

Transparencies

In the classified catalogue, entries for all types of materials are integrated in a single sequence, so that the use of form divisions would present unwanted subsidiary sequences. The form of material is clearly indicated within the catalogue entry and the shelving sequence is indicated by a location mark before the class number (see figure two).

The major problem in using DC (or any other conventional classification) is that the broad topics studied in schools often do not conform to the subject analysis in classification schemes. For example material may be required on 'water', which in DC may be classified at several places including 333.339 (Economic control of water), 333.91 (Utilization of water), 338.456281 (Economics of the water supply industry), 338.76281 (Organizations in the water supply industry), 352.6 (Local government control of water supply), 386 (Inland waterway transportation), 387 (Water, air, space transportation), 546.22 (Chemistry of water), 551.4 (Geomorphology), 551.524 (water temperature), 574.92 (Marine biology), 581.92 (Marine botany), 591.92 (Marine zoology), 614.772 (Public health aspects of water pollution), 614.81 (Water safety), 628.1 (Water supply), 631.7 (Irrigation and water conservation), 714 (Water features in landscape design), 797 (Aquatic and air sports) and 910.02 (Physical geography).

Similarly schools may initiate projects on countries, scattered by subject in all classification schemes, and on periods such as the Renaissance or the nineteenth century.

One solution to this problem is the preparation of charts showing the interrelationships of DC class numbers within broad themes. Another is to regard classification purely as a shelving device, relying on detailed subject indexing for information retrieval. This is one reason why PRECIS was introduced into the Library in December 1976 after earlier experiments (see page 157).

Another method used to overcome this problem of 'broad themes' and 'distributed relatives' is the publication of 'materiographies' on

27

S
917. AMERICAN Museum in
      Britain, Bath. — London:
300   Trans-Globe, [n.d.] — (R760)
740
238   SLIDESET. 5x5cm: 5 slides:
        col.
      Contents: Claverton Manor —
      Perley Parlour — Deer Park
      Parlour — Pennsylvania /
      Dutch exhibit — Milliner's
      shop. — Available also as
      individual slides.
                      MCN.003297

S
917. The AMERICAN Museum in
      Britain, Bath. —
300   London: Trans-Globe, [n.d.].
      — (R770)
740
238   SLIDESET. 5x5cm: 5 slides:
        col.
      Contents: Claverton Manor —
      Deming Parlour — Conkeys
      Tavern — Shaker exhibit —
      New Orleans bedroom. —
      Available also as single slides.
                      MCN.003294

S
917. FOLK art: American Museum
      in Britain, Bath. —
300   London: Trans-Globe, [n.d.].
      — (P.420).
740
238   SLIDESET. 5x5cm: 5 slides:
        col.
      Also available as individual
      slides.
                      MCN.003296

S
917. HOOKED rugs: American
      Museum in Britain, Bath.
300   London: Trans-Globe, [n.d.].
740   — (P400).
238

Figure 2: Extract from a materiography on the USA.
ILEA Centre for Learning Resources

such subjects as Power and Energy, Africa, the United States of America, Birds, Environmental experience and Community help. For example a materiography on Environmental experience, published in November 1975, lists 154 items (books, pamphlets, slides, cardsets, discs, filmstrips, portfolios, audiotapes, games, filmloops, charts and picture sets) classified at 001.56, 082, 301, 301.1, 301.3, 301.31, 301.32, 301.34, 301.35, 301.36, 301.54, 333.7, 338, 338.1, 372.83, 372.89, 380.5, 381, 381.416, 382.4, 385, 386, 386.4, 387, 388.1, 388.31, 523.1, 526.8, 553, 574.526, 574.52636, 574.5264, 574.543, 574.9, 574.92, 581.133, 622.33, 625.7, 636, 696, 711.4, 711.55, 711.58, 711.7, 711.73, 711.74, 719, 719.32, 720, 726.5, 728, 728.3, 728.81, 745.4, 808 and 914.23. An example from a materiography on the United States of America is reproduced as figure two.

DC in school libraries

I have deliberately chosen to include a number of school libraries in this book because so many librarians fail to appreciate that such libraries need efficient classification and indexing systems to cope with subject enquiries and project work. The excellent books by Shifrin[9] and Beswick[10] should now have done something to demonstrate this need.

Another point to bear in mind is that many school libraries, though as large as some public branch libraries, may have to manage with one qualified librarian and minimal clerical help. In some respects the school library resembles the industrial special library, with the one librarian working under intense pressure during term time attempting to cope with the demands of teachers and pupils. As one whose knowledge of school librarianship is limited, I was very impressed by the dynamism and enthusiasm of the staff in the school libraries which I visited.

Codsall High School, near Wolverhampton

The six schools surveyed by Beswick for the Schools Council's Resource Centre project[10] all used DC. One of these, Codsall High School, uses the ninth abridged edition for books, supported where necessary by entries in an optical coincidence card index (see pages 170-3). In spite of the well-known disadvantages of DC, such as the scattering of geography, it is felt desirable that pupils should become familiar with a scheme which they are going to meet in their public library (unless they move to Edinburgh) and which they stand a fair chance of meeting in their institute of higher education.

For sixth form economics students there is also a classified index in book form using the full eighteenth edition, listing articles, pamphlets and sections of books. The following is a typical entry:

STRIKES   331.892
'*The Advisory, Conciliation and Arbitration Service*', Article
    Department of Employment News no 20, March 1975
'The Trade Unions' by Hugh Williamson. Book. 331.8
    Strikes. p 37-49, 111-112, 117-118
'*Days Lost. Lowest in 7 Years*'. Article
    Department of Employment News no 29, 1976

St Thomas the Apostle School, Peckham, London
    The library of St Thomas the Apostle School, Peckham, uses the
ninth abridged edition of DC for all library materials, which are integrated in the catalogue but not on the shelves where there are separate
sequences for books, wallcharts, records, 'Jackdaws', kits, overhead
projector transparencies, slides, cassettes and tapes, filmstrips, film
loops, videotapes and videocassettes. The classification works satisfactorily except that the class numbers are sometimes too broad for the
retrieval of specific items of information.
    The problem of 'distributed relatives' is overcome by the use of
chain indexing, which allows a pupil doing a project quickly to locate
materials on all aspects of a topic. For example a pupil doing a project
on oil will first consult the subject index, where he will find
    Oil
        Geology   553
        Industry: Economics 338.2
        Mining   622
        Products   665
Consulting the classified catalogue at 665 he will find a number of
entries including
    665   TOOLEY, P
                    Fats, oils and waxes.
                    1971.
                8532
    665   VEGETABLE OILS.
                    (Our Changing World series. Tape 18.)
                        BBC. AUT. '76
                            T. 20 mins. 4". 3-3/4ips. TN. PN.
                1781
(In the above example, T indicates tape, TN means that there are
teachers' notes and PN means that there are pupils' notes).
    Further information about each item is given on the accession cards,
which are filed in accession number order. This information includes
order details, vendor and binding information for books and level (first
year, second year, third year, fourth year, fifth year, sixth year or
staff) for audio-visual materials.

Parliament Hill School, London

Parliament Hill School uses the seventh abridged edition of DC, supplemented where necessary by the tenth abridged edition, for all material including books, slides, packs (such as 'Jackdaws'), discs, games, kits, audio-tapes, overhead projector transparencies, postcards, cassettes, videotapes, charts and project material (ie ephemeral material such as news cuttings, pamphlets and the Sunday newspaper colour supplements).

The major problem of DC for school libraries — that of 'distributed relatives'—is solved by collecting all aspects of a topic at one class number: for example, everything on transport is collected at 625 (385 being unused), everything on the role of women at 301.424 (396 being unused), everything on children at 302 (362.7 and 649 being unused) and everything on geography at 910. 380.9 (Commercial geography) is unused and the following additions are made at 910:

910.1   Commodities
910.2   Distribution

Some adjustments are also made in the shelving of material, with the use of broken order to collocate related topics: 910 (Geography) is followed by 909 (General history) and 940-999 (Modern history by locality), and Ancient history (930) is shelved with Classical mythology (290).

Cataloguing and classification are deliberately kept simple, but subject enquiries are catered for by the liberal use of added entries as can be seen from the following selections from the 'slavery' section of the classified catalogue:

Subject index
SLAVERY   326
Classified catalogue
326
The abolition of the slave trade (SLIDESET).
Education Productions, 1973.
Set of 12 slides, notes

—

(326)
AUGIER, F R & GORDON, Shirley C, compilers
Sources of West Indian history. 1962.
MAIN ENTRY: 972.9

—

326
CHAPMAN, Abraham, ed
Steal away: slaves tell their own stories.
Benn, 1973. £1.75

—

326
LANGDON-DAVIES, John
The slave trade and its abolition. (PACK)
80p.
Jackdaw 12

—

(326)
MEDIA RESOURCES CENTRE
Black studies. MRC, 1972 (PACK)
SHELVED AT: 325

Hazel Grove High School, Stockport
Hazel Grove High School has used DC18 for its bookstock since the new library opened in September 1974. Previously the tenth abridged edition had been used, but with the envisaged expansion of library facilities and the wider curriculum of a comprehensive school, it was considered that the detail of the eighteenth edition was desirable in certain subject areas, especially sociology, psychology, chemistry and parts of biology, zoology and engineering.

Few amendments are made to the official schedules, but much of the detail provided is ignored. Social surveys are shelved at history rather than with social sciences, thus providing what is regarded as a more convenient arrangement as well as a shorter notation, but added entries are made in the classified catalogue, thus:

309.142.081
shelved at
942.081

ALLEN, Eleanor
Victorian children. A & C Black, 1973.
Also, the original classification of biography at 920-929 is retained, rather than classification by subject as recommended in the eighteenth edition. This does not always meet with the approval of the teaching staff, who would prefer all biographies of composers (for example) to be at music, but the librarian points out that it is sometimes difficult to assign a single class number for biographies under subject. (This could also apply to classification at 920-929, of course, and is why many libraries prefer to arrange biographies alphabetically by biographee.)

Another interesting amendment occurs at 373 (secondary education), where the geographical divisions (373.3/373.9) are ignored and the notations used instead to represent teaching of specific subjects, dividing like 372.3/.8. Strict application of DC would place such books with their subjects, and the following examples illustrate the two approaches:

32

	Hazel Grove	DC
Books for the retarded reader	373.413	428.420712
Starting points for teaching mathematics in middle and secondary schools	373.7	510.712
Projects in history	373.89	907.12

On the whole it is considered that DC works very well, but there is the inevitable 'distributed relatives' problem such as the separation of electricity (537) from electrical engineering (621.3) and transport economics (385/388) from transport engineering (625/629). Although DC18 goes some way towards alleviating the 'geography' problem by placing physical geography at 910.02, it is still not regarded as satisfactory and there remains the unfortunate separation of geography of specific localities (914/919) from their history (940/999).

DC is not used for audio-visual materials, although the librarian believes it would cope as satisfactorily with most of them as the post-co-ordinate indexing system which is in use (see pages 173-6).

The British Library (Library Association Library)

The final case study is a special library. The Library Association library used mainly the sixteenth edition of DC until 1966, when it was decided to adopt the *Classification of library science* devised by the Classification Research Group (Preliminary edition, London, Aslib, 1965.) DC was readopted (this time the eighteenth edition) from September 1976 onwards for two major reasons. First, the revision of the CRG classification (now called *Classification of library and information science*—see pages 133-5) was not considered entirely satisfactory and was completely incompatible with the version in use. Secondly, since the appearance of the revision made reclassification essential, it was considered that the library (now administered by the British Library) should conform to national and international standards by adopting DC as on MARC records.

The aim of speeding-up processing by taking DC numbers from MARC records has not been completely achieved, because 'teething troubles' meant that records were not received as quickly as had been hoped. It has also been found that class numbers on UK MARC records are not always acceptable as they stand: for example, school resource centres are classified with school libraries at 027.8 by the Library Association library but with education, at 371.3078, on UK MARC records. There is also some confusion between library management (at 658.9102) and library administration (at 025.1). The Library Association library does not find it desirable to follow the UK MARC practice of classifying library catalogues under type of library instead of at subject bibliography: for example *Derbyshire: books and*

33

other materials available in the county library published by Derbyshire County Library in 1971, was classified by UK MARC at 026.914251 (special libraries on Derbyshire topography) rather than 016.914251 (bibliographies of Derbyshire topography). However the Library Association library is accepting nearly all class numbers as they occur in UK MARC.

A further problem is that class numbers on LC MARC records are not always compatible with those on UK MARC records. Also, the library acquires a great deal of foreign language material and unpublished material which is not yet covered by either UK MARC or LC MARC.

The following table shows the number of items classified by UK MARC, LC MARC and the Library Association library itself from September to November 1976:

	Current additions			Recataloguing		
	UK MARC	LC MARC	LA	UK MARC	LC MARC	TOTAL
13.9.76	6	6	14	80	—	106
26.10.76	24	12	74	—	—	110
22.11.76	37	32	113	2	—	184
Total September–November 1976	67	50	201	82		400

As a general scheme, DC cannot of course provide anything like the detail which was possible when using the CRG scheme. To take a very simple example, an item on cataloguing in public libraries could only be classified by DC at cataloguing (025.3) or public libraries (027.4)—it is impossible to specify both facets.

Dewey outside Britain and North America

Downing,[1] Batty[11] and Vann[12] have shown that the use of DC is by no means confined to the United States, Britain and Canada. Downing comments on efforts made since the sixteenth edition to increase the usefulness of DC outside North America, such as the introduction and extension of the area tables; tables for racial, ethnic and national groups; optional devices such as those in Law, Religion, and Customs; and the development of international co-operation. He points out that it is now used in the national bibliographies of Argentina, Brazil, Denmark, Egypt, Ethiopia, France, Iceland, India, Iran, Italy, the Ivory Coast, Malaysia, Norway, Rhodesia, Sierra Leone, Singapore, South Africa, Tanzania and Turkey. It is used by all French public libraries, as well as by the Bibliothèque Nationale, and the French translation (published in 1975) is also used in Quebec. In addition to the full French translation, there have been authorized translations in abridged versions published in Icelandic, Indonesian, Japanese, Korean, Malay, Norwegian, Turkish and Vietnamese and a selective abridgement in Hindi with expansions in special areas. A Spanish translation is being prepared.

Batty comments on the wide use of DC in Indian libraries in spite of the existence of Ranganathan's Colon Classification, which makes special provision for Indian needs. He also reports on surveys in Australia (1972) and New Zealand (1973). In the Australian survey, eighty-seven of ninety-eight responding libraries were using DC, including all public libraries and state cataloguing agencies. A study of 247 New Zealand libraries again showed that all public libraries were using DC but the overall percentage (54.51) was much lower than the 88.77 per cent in the Australian survey.

Friis-Hansen[13] reports that the first edition of the Danish Decimal Classification (DK1) was published by the State Inspectorate for Public Libraries in 1915, emanating from the seventh edition of DC (1911) but reducing its 800 pages to fifty-one, and also collocating language and literature.[14] The fourth edition (1954) and the fifth edition (1970) were published by the Library Bureau. Friss-Hansen gives no figures for use but the fact that five editions have been published is a clear indication of its popularity.

A survey by the Norwegian Classification Committee in 1975, indicated that sixty-one of 320 libraries, mainly in the fields of science and technology, were using DC. There is a trend from the UDC and the University of Oslo system (UBO) towards DC, and 1,300 Norwegian public libraries are known to use DC.[15]

Mrs J D Hill has described the partial reclassification of Johannesburg Public Library from the DC16 to DC18, largely as a result of frequent use of BNB.[16] She mentions some of the problems involved including the need to move books from one subject library to another, for example flower arranging from 635.9663 (in the Reference Library) to 745.92 (in the Arts Library) and microfilming from 778.315 (in the Photographic Library) to 686.43 (in the Reference Library). She also comments on the movement of rural life from 630.1 to the 910s and quotes the staggering class number given to Ronald Blythe's *Akenfield*— 914.264203850922, representing a collection of personal observations on twentieth century civilization in East Suffolk. Other problems include archaeology, computers, the poor index and the occasional provision of more than one class number for the same subject.

Conclusion

In 1967 Ben Custer, current editor of DC, wrote an article entitled 'Dewey lives'.[17] These two words are obviously still true today, and the widespread acceptance of DC is due in no small measure to two people. Custer himself has brought many modern ideas of classification to the pioneer scheme and so made it a suitable tool for libraries of all kinds. And Joel Downing, Chairman of the (British) Library Association Research Committee's Dewey Decimal Classification

Subcommittee, has done a great deal to transmit the views of British users and, with Custer, to stimulate international co-operation in the development of DC.

References
1 Downing, Joel C 'The DDC: the classification upon which the sun never sets' *Wilson Library bulletin* 50(1) June 1976, 797-800.

2 Adams, Melba Davis 'Application of the Dewey Decimal Classification at the British National Bibliography' *Library resources and technical services* 19(1) winter 1975, 35-40.

3 Bruin, Joyce, E 'The practice of classification: a study towards standardization' *Journal of librarianship* 3(1) January 1971, 60-71.

4 Trotter, Robert Ross 'Application of the Dewey Decimal Classification at the Library of Congress' *Library resources and technical services* 19(1) winter 1975, 41-45.

5 Comaromi, John P; Michael, Mary Ellen; and Bloom, Janet *A survey of the use of the Dewey Decimal Classification in the United States and Canada* Lake Placid Foundation, Forest Press, 1975.

6 Sweeney, Russell 'Dewey in Britain' *Catalogue and index* (30) summer 1973, 4-6, 15.

7 British Library, Working Party on Classification and Indexing *Final report* Boston Spa, British Library, 1975. (British Library Research and Development Report no 5233) p 13, para 26.

8 Shifrin, Malcolm 'The library and information service at the ILEA's Media Resources Centre: a personal view' *Education libraries bulletin* 18(2) summer 1975, 21-30.

9 Shifrin, Malcolm *Information in the school library: an introduction to the organization of non-book materials* London, Bingley, 1973.

10 Beswick, Norman *Organizing resources: six case-studies: the final report of the Schools Council Resource Centre Project* London, Heinemann Educational, 1975.

11 Batty, David 'Dewey abroad: the international use of the Dewey Decimal Classification' *Quarterly journal of the Library of Congress* 33(4) October 1976, 300-310.

12 Vann, Sarah K 'Dewey decimal classification' (in Maltby, pp 226-255).

13 Friis-Hansen, J B 'Library classification systems in Denmark' *International classification* 3(2) 1976, 91-93.

14 Friis-Hansen, J B 'What Dewey knew' *Libri* 26(3) September 1976, 216-230.
15 Personal communication from Tor Henriksen
16 Hill, J D 'The use of the 18th edition of Dewey in the Johannesburg Public Library' *South African libraries* 42(5) April 1985, 187-189.
17 Custer, Benjamin A 'Dewey lives' *Library resources and technical services* 11(1) winter 1967, 51-60.

For further information about DC see Foskett chapter seventeen, and Maltby/Sayers chapter nine.

Chapter Two

THE UNIVERSAL DECIMAL CLASSIFICATION

THE UNIVERSAL DECIMAL CLASSIFICATION (UDC) was a direct result of an international conference held at Brussels in 1895, from which sprang the Institut International de la Bibliographie, later to become the Institut International de la Documentation, and then Fédération International de Documentation (FID). At this 1895 conference two Belgians—Paul Otlet and Henri La Fontaine—called for a card index of world literature, for the arrangement of which a detailed international classification was needed. Dewey's permission to extend and adapt DC was sought and granted, subject to there being no major structural changes. Although the card catalogue had to be abandoned in the 1920s, UDC continued to flourish.

The first full edition was published in French in 1905. A full English edition has been promised for many years, but there are still a number of classes not available and several of those which have been published are now woefully out of date. A list of available schedules appears in *British standards yearbook*, published by the British Standards Institution.

Many libraries in Britain and other English-speaking countries make use of the English abridgment (3rd ed, BS1000A, 1961), supplemented where appropriate by expanded schedules for individual classes. The existence of a trilingual abridgment in French, English and German (BS1000B, 1958) facilitates classification of foreign language material, though obviously these schedules are now much out of date. A medium edition, containing approximately one-third of the material in the full edition, has been published in some languages. We are still awaiting the English medium edition, although it was promised for 1976 (DC centenary year).

The major change from DC lies in the notation. The three-figure minimum of Dewey was abolished, so that Science (for example) is now 5 instead of 500 and Chemistry is 54 instead of 540. More important, there are many auxiliary signs and symbols (eg : to indicate relationship, (0) to indicate form, (3/9) to indicate place and " " to indicate period). These allow much greater specificity but also complicate the notation.

The order and collocation of DC and UDC are substantially the same, though a notable change occurred in 1964 when UDC abolished class 4 and moved Language to the Literature class at 8.07. Porter has commented on the improved classification for the professional geographer provided by the expanded class 91, published in 1973, while regretting that it did not take more account of the International Geographical Union's extended systematic outline.[1]

UDC is often regarded as a technology-biased scheme but it is in fact a *general* classification. Of the four British case studies dealt with here, one is a 'non-technical' special library (the British Institute of Management) and another is a university (Bath) which, although originally a technological university, is now also strong in the humanities and social sciences.

University of Bath

One reason given by the librarian of the University of Bath for the adoption of UDC is that it was the cheapest classification scheme available! It was also the most suitable scheme for the stock, which had a technological bias when the university was formed in 1966, and it was used in a number of similar universities.

The abridged schedules (BS100A: 1961) are used as the basis of the classification, supplemented where appropriate by expanded schedules. These schedules are not, however, used without amendment. The most frequently used auxiliary symbols are the colon (to link two or more subjects) and the place divisions. The period divisions have been gradually withdrawn and have been replaced in History by the use of DC. The point of view numbers (.00) were originally used a great deal but are now used very sparingly. Some members of the library staff have requested less use of the hyphen and the oblique stroke, but the latter has a particular value for combining consecutive notations to specify 'general' subjects which would not otherwise be classifiable (eg 361/362 Social work). Very little use is made of the plus sign, form divisions, (=) to represent race or = to represent language. There is a three-figure minimum in the notation (as in Dewey), so that science is 500 and not 5.

The major changes to the structure of the scheme concern the Language and Literature classes (400 and 800), both of which have been revised, in collaboration with the academic staff of the university, to provide a more effective order together with the required detail and a simpler notation. The following extracts from the revised schedule for French language, which was largely the work of Mr J C Smith, a lecturer in the School of Modern Languages, indicate some of the differences from BS1000A. All other languages are treated at Bath in the same manner.

Bath		BS1000A
44R	Romance languages	44/46
440	French language	440
440.4	Foreign influences on French	–
441	Minimal units or building blocks of French (spoken and written)	–
441.1	Phonetics	440-4
441.11	Articulatory phonetics	–
441.12	Acoustic phonetics	–
441.13	Auditory phonetics	–
441.7	Alphabet	440-1.1
441.72	Spelling, orthography	440-1
441.77	Writing	840.081
441.78	Punctuation	–
442.2	Synonyms	440-3.14
442.21	Antonyms	–
442.3	Vocabulary in general	030.8=44?
442.31	Word formation	440-13?
442.32	Neologisms	440-3.16
442.34	Foreign influences on vocabulary: loan-words	440-3.163
442.35	Learned words (use of Latin, Greek etc)	440-3.163
442.36	Terminology	440-3.164
442.38	Geographical proper names	440-3.11
442.39	Personal names, surnames etc	440-3.13
442.7	Locutions, idioms	440-3.18
442.9	Etymology	440-3.2
447	Non-standard French. Styles and registers of French in general	449?
447.01	Old French (824-1400)	440"824/1400"
447.02	Middle French (1400-1600)	440"1400/1600"
447.03	Seventeenth century ('classical' or 'early modern') French	440"16"
447.1	Social variation in general (esp popular French)	–

Bath		BS1000A
447.11	Slang	440-09.3
447.2	Linguistic geography	—
447.23	Linguistic atlases	440(084.4)
447.3	Dialects in general	440-08.7
447.39	Franco-provençal	449.0
447.4	French outside France	—
447.5	Artificial forms of French — le Français fundamental	440-08.9
448	French usage. Prescriptive and normative grammar	440-5
448.02	Translation into French	840.03
448.028	Machine translation	—
448.03	Interpreting into French	840.03
448.2	Language textbooks for foreign students	—
448.3	Use of words, conversation primers	—
448.4	Reading. Remedial reading. Developmental reading (ie increased efficiency, faster reading)	?
449	Occitan (inc Provençal, Gascon etc)	447.7/.8

In Literature too the notation has been simplified by the removal of the hyphen to indicate form. The following examples show Bath's amendments and the 'official' BS1000A.

800	Literature in general	8
801	Literature, theory and philosophy	—
803	Literary translation—general	8.03
808	Literary technique, technical writing, rhetoric	8.08
808.066	Commercial or business letter composition—general	8-6
808.1	Literary style	8.081
808.5	Elocution, voice production	8.085.1
808.54	Lecturing technique	8.085.4
808.88	Quotations	—
809	Literary criticism—general	8.09
810	Literary forms—general	8-1/-9
811	Poetry as a literary form	8-1
812	Drama as a literary form	8-2

813	Prose (incl fiction) as a literary form	8-3
814	Essays as a literary form	8-4
815	Speeches and letters as a literary form	8-5 (speeches) 8-6 (letters)
816	Satire and humour as a literary form	8-7

Anthologies and critical studies of specific literary forms
(Auxiliaries of time " " can be applied before .09)

830	Anthologies of German literature by several authors	830(082)
830(03)	Encyclopaedias of German literature	830(03)
830.09	Critical study of German literature	830.09
831	Anthology of German poetry	830-1(082)
831(03)	Encyclopaedia of German poetry	830-1(03)
831.09	Critical study of German poetry	830-1.09
832	Anthology of German drama	830-2(082)
833	Anthology of German prose	830-3(082)
834	Anthology of German essays	830-4(082)
835	Anthology of German letters and speeches	830-5(082) 830-6(082)
836	Anthology of German satire and humour	830-7(082)

(832/836 subdivided as 830 and 831)

837	Works of individual authors, arranged alphabetically

eg

837 GOE	Goethe's works, whatever their form and whether in the original German or in translation
837 GOE.09	Critical studies of Goethe

All other literatures are treated in the same way as German. It will be seen that form and period are ignored for individual authors, as an alphabetical arrangement (following general collections and studies of the literature) is considered more helpful to users of the library. It will also be noticed that Bath has not moved Language to class 8 in accordance with the change made by UDC in 1961, though Language and Literature are shelved together.

Other schedules which have been completely revised include 360 (Social welfare) and 370 (Education). An example from the latter indicates the problems which can arise through slow revision of UDC and relocation when revisions appear. In BS1000A, Education of special categories of pupils is classified at 371.9 without subdivision, and Bath has produced its own expansion with, for example, Education of delinquents at 371.93, Education of problem children at 371.94 and Education of immigrants at 371.97. In the English expansion of class 37, published in 1975, Special school education is moved to the previously unused 376, with Education of delinquents at 376.58, Education of problem children at 376.5 and Education of immigrants at 376.684.

Class 330 (Economics) is considered unsatisfactory and is being revised at Bath, the cross-classification between 331 (Labour), 338 (Production) and parts of 650 (Management) being particularly bad. Class 380 (Commerce and trade) has been abolished and a new expansion for commerce and trade is being created at 330.3. All works on management are placed at 658 (Business, works and shop management and techniques), thus avoiding confusion between this and 650 (Management), which is unused.

Non-book materials are classified in exactly the same way as books and all materials are integrated in the catalogue.

UDC is not liked by users—staff or students—mainly because of its complex notation and the problem of filing order associated with the auxiliary signs and symbols. Confusion may also result from the frequent use of two class numbers: there is a limitation of eight digits in the name catalogue and on the spine of each document, but the class number used for the classified catalogue is as full as is considered necessary for the retrieval of specific items of information. Often, therefore, the filing number in the classified catalogue is different from the number at which the document is shelved, as in the following example:

159.922.7:170   Moral learning and development   159.922.7
1972 (Graham, D)

The classified catalogue is supported by a chain index, so that the above item receives the following subject index entries:

Moral learning: Child psychology	159.922.7:170
Child psychology	159.922.7
Individuation: Developmental psychology	159.922
Developmental psychology	159.92
Psychology	159.9

Students appear to prefer using the KWOC index, however, for retrieval of subject information (see page 167).

The British Institute of Management

UDC has been used by the British Institute of Management Library since its formation in 1947. A number of other schemes were examined, notably the Bliss Bibliographic Classification, and Derek Langridge—then in charge of cataloguing at BIM, now a principal lecturer at the Polytechnic of North London's School of Librarianship—compiled a faceted classification for management literature. UDC was chosen, although not a particularly suitable scheme for management, for a number of reasons including its popularity in British special libraries and the fact that, at that time, its future seemed assured.

The 1961 abridged English edition is now used in the library, supplemented by home-made expansions in the management area. Particularly interesting are the schedules for personnel management, which bring together and expand UDC's 331 (Industrial relations) and 658.3 (Personnel management) schedules, using the notation M3 and thus reducing the UDC notation by two digits. Extracts from the schedules appear below together with the 'official' UDC class numbers for comparison.

BIM		UDC
M311.01	Manpower planning	658.3.012.2
M312	Recruitment	331.115.1 & 658.311
M312.1	Recruiting bureaux	331.115.11
M312.12	Labour exchanges (state)	331.115.11
M312.13	Appointments boards	?
M312.14	Agencies (private)	331.115.11 & 658.311.511
M312.15	Youth Employment Service	?
M312.2	Situations vacant notices	331.115.12
M312.21	Internal advertising of positions vacant	331.115.12
M312.3	Liaison with schools	?
M312.4	Liaison with professional bodies	?
M312.5	Vocational guidance	371.425
M312.54	Placement	?
M312.6	Recruiting brochures. Careers	?
M312.7	Film features	?
M312.8	Community surveys	?
M331	Wage structure	331.2
M331.1	Job evaluation	65.015.3
M331.11	Familiarity rating	?
M331.2	Job classification and grading	65.015.3
M331.4	Wage scales and rates	658.32.03

BIM		UDC
M371	Trade unionism	331.881
M371.1	Development	331.881(09)
M371.2	Union structure	331.881.2
M371.3	Representatives (shop stewards)	331.881.2?
M371.4	Restrictive practices	?
M371.41	Demarcation rules	?
M371.42	Feather bedding	?
M371.5	Closed shop. Union shop. Agency shop.	?
M38	Education and vocational training	658.386
M386	Management training. Executive development	658.386-052.2
M386.1	Firms' schemes	658.386-052.2
M386.2	Institutional	658.386-052.2
M387	Top management. Multiple management	658.386-052.2
M387.1	Firms' schemes. Junior boards	658.386-052.2
M387.2	Institutional	658.386-052.2

The English edition of the management expansion (65), published in 1968, was not adopted by BIM partly because of the amount of re-classification which would have been involved and partly because the librarian—like many others—was not particularly impressed by it.

A classified catalogue is maintained, with rotation of entries preferred to chain indexing in the case of compound subjects. Thus, a case study of financial management in an international clothing materials company is classified at M38.022.5:658.115.2:658.15:687.053, where M38.022.5 represents case studies, 658.115.2 is international operations, 658.15 is financial management and 687.053 is clothing materials manufacture. Added entries are provided in the catalogue at 658.115.2, 658.15 and 687.053. This means four entries in the classified catalogue, each class number having its own subject index entries. The use of chain indexing for the whole string would have resulted in only *one* entry in the classified catalogue, supported by the following index entries:

Clothing industries: Financial management:
International management: Case studies
        M38.022.5:658.115.2:658.15:687.053
Financial management: International management:
Case studies   M38.022.5:658.115.2:658.15
International management: Case studies   M38.022.5:658.115.2
Case studies   M38.022.5

Clearly the use of chain procedure for composite class marks would result in economies in typing and filing and also a reduction in the size of the classified file, but there are obvious advantages in being able to locate everything on financial management at 658.15, everything on international management at 658.115.2, etc.

Because of this desire to be able to locate everything at one place in the classified file, the colon is always preferred to the use of form divisions. For example an encyclopedia of management is classified at 03:658 rather than 658(03), giving it two entries in the classified catalogue. Because of the frequency of requests for information on management problems in particular countries, a geographical file is also maintained with the locality number filing before the class number, as in the following example:

PM361(430.1)(485)(497.1)(41-4)

SHUTT, Harry *ed*
Worker participation in West Germany, Sweden, Yugoslavia and the United Kingdom.
London, Economist Intelligence Unit, 1957.
48p, diagrs. (QER Special no 20)

(430.1), indicating West Germany, is underlined to indicate that this is the part of the notation under which the card is filed, and additional entries are provided for (485) (Sweden), (497.1) (Yugoslavia) and (41-4) (United Kingdom).

The present librarian of BIM, Gillian Dare, sees as the main advantage of UDC the closeness of classification which is possible, allowing speedy retrieval of items on very specific subjects. The main disadvantage is the well-known one of complicated notation with no obvious filing order of symbols. Readers also fail to appreciate the hierarchical structure of the notation, although there is a very useful guide to this at the catalogue (see figure three). This hierarchical structure is a great advantage to the library staff when carrying out searches: if there is no material on hiring or renting at 658.729.3, the search can be broadened to 658.729 (Purchasing leasing and hiring), 658.72 (Purchasing methods) and 658.7 (Purchasing).

The flexibility of UDC, with no prescribed citation order, is both an advantage and a disadvantage. It is up to the librarian to decide whether a book on job evaluation for supervisors is more appropriately classed at Job evaluation or Supervision and this means that the most appropriate collocation for the library can be used. It can also result in some inconsistency if decisions are not carefully recorded, and this has occasionally happened at BIM. For example, although all encyclopedias are preferred at 03, Oliver Standingford's *Encyclopedia of business management* has been classified at 658:03.

46

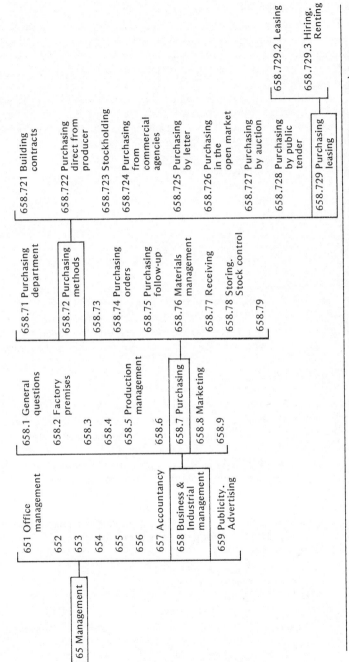

Figure 3: Hierarchy in the Universal Decimal Classification (Guide at the British Institute of Management)

University of Bradford

The University of Bradford uses the UDC English abridgement for science and technology only. A simplified version is used, auxiliary signs and symbols being kept to a minimum: the colon (for relationship) and the brackets (for form or geographical subdivision) are the most used symbols.

The initial classification at Bradford into twenty-five broad subject groupings corresponding to the university's teaching interests (see page 17) has the advantage of bringing together aspects of a subject which have been separated in UDC, as in the following example:

X	Civil engineering. Building. Architecture
X528	Surveying. Geodesy
X624	Civil engineering
X69	Building
X71	Town and country planning
X72	Architecture

An additional use of UDC at Bradford is to provide an added entry for all non-book materials in the classified catalogue under the UDC class number representing its form. For example *Guide to literature searching techniques: case study in sulphur dioxide pollution*, a tape-slide presentation produced by the University of Bradford library, is classified at A029.954622400931 (the letter A for General works followed by the appropriate Dewey number) with an added entry at A045:029, 045 being the UDC notation for tape-slide presentations.

ICI Fibres, Harrogate

UDC has been used in the library of ICI Fibres, Harrogate, since the 1950s. For books the abridged edition is used, with only a very limited application of the auxiliary signs and symbols and some deviations from normal practice such as the classification of all dictionaries and encyclopedias at (03) rather than by subject because it is more useful to collect such works on the shelves rather than to scatter them by subject. For example, *Handbook of chemistry and physics* is classified at (03)5.

For periodical articles much more detailed classification is practised, using specially prepared schedules. The following examples show the ICI notation and the UDC abridgement (BS1000A) notation.

ICI Fibres		BS1000A
677	Textile industries	677
677.00	Textile industries in general	677.01
677.01	Properties of textiles	677.014
677.015.42	Strength of textiles	677.014:620.1
677.02	Textile processes	677.02

ICI Fibres		BS1000A
677.04	Textile auxiliaries	677.04
677.044.78	Pigments	677.021.122.45?
677.05	Textile machinery	677.05
677.051.5	Spinning machinery	677.052.3/.5
677.07	Textile products	677.06
677.072	Yarns	677.061
677.076.23	Lace	677.653
677.1	Fibres in general	677-1
677.4	Synthetic fibres	677.494
677.5	Mineral fibres	677.51/.53
677.51	Cotton fibres	—

Some combined numbers are quite formidable, for example
677.027.3: 677.494.674'044.4 Dyeing polyester fibres with vat dyes,
or
677.027.3:677.494.674'044.4P Pad cake dyeing of polyester fibres
with vat dyes.

Subarrangement within class numbers is chronological, the least
recent items being filed first.

UDC and computers: Europe

Van Helm has described the use of UDC in a KWIC index for selective dissemination of information at the Central Information Department of Bronswerk NV, Amersfoort, Netherlands.[2] The main reasons
for choosing UDC were the facts that a) it is language-independent, thus
facilitating international exchange of information, and b) it lends itself
to mechanization. Depth classification is used because it was felt
desirable to spend time and money at the input stage thus ensuring
immediate enquiry response and preventing waiting time.

The Bronswerk UDC/QUIC system (BUQ), based on an IBM/KWIC
index, uses terms from the UDC schedules as well as from titles of
documents for supplying information based on user profiles. Alphabetical and classified listing are provided.

Also in the Netherlands, Kien has reported on efforts to correlate
the Library of Congress subject headings with the third English
abridged edition of UDC because of the need to classify titles systematically as part of PICA (Project for Integrated Catalogue Automation).[3]
Unfortunately there has been little progress on this work since 1971.[4]

The Technological University Library of Denmark received a grant
from the IBM Research Foundation in 1967 for developing a program
for the production of library catalogues for its own library and departmental libraries.[5] In 1970 the library, which acts as a central research
library for Danish industry and the technological community as a

whole, began to distribute book catalogues of its collections.[6] The computerized system can handle catalogue production for ninety-nine libraries. It uses all the auxiliary symbols except " " (period), = (language) and ' (special analytical for chemistry).

Other computerized applications in the Netherlands and Denmark have been reported by Rigby, who also describes developments in Belgium, France, Germany, Hungary, Italy, Poland, Switzerland, the USSR and the United Kingdom.[7]

UDC and computers: the United States and Canada

Although pioneered by two Europeans and developed in Europe, UDC has always been an international classification. One major project which links Europe and the United States is the establishment by the International Federation for Documentation (FID), The Hague, and the US National Federation of Abstracting and Indexing Services (NFAIS), Philadelphia, of a joint data base covering indexing and abstracting services in all fields of knowledge.[8] UDC numbers are assigned to the data base by FID and the tapes for the base are retained in both Philadelphia and the Hague for searching. Indexes are generated by country, language, institute and subject.

Some of the most interesting mechanized experiments and applications have taken place in the United States, the Freeman/Atherton investigations for the American Institute of Physics[9] being particularly significant. The practical results of this major project have included the development of a machine-readable file of UDC schedules for mechanized UDC file maintenance, automatic typesetting and composition of UDC schedules, keyboarding UDC schedules, and the statistical evaluation of UDC as a retrieval tool. Project AUDACIOUS (Automatic Direct Access to Information with On-line UDC System) was one of the most interesting parts of the Freeman and Atherton research: an experimental system for remote direct access to files of computer-stored information consisting of 2330 items from one issue of *Nuclear science abstracts* indexed by UDC, this was claimed to be the first on-line interactive retrieval system to use one of the traditional classification schemes.

The American Meteorological Institute has also done a great deal of work linking UDC with computerized retrieval, including the production of a fifteen-year concordance of subject headings from *Meteorological and geoastrophysical abstracts* with equivalent UDC numbers; a computerized *Meteorological and geoastrophysical titles*, arranged in UDC order; computerized production of multilingual UDC schedules and an English-language schedule; production of an open-ended multi-access indexing system for abstracts or titles on satellite meteorology; and a quarterly accessions list for the National Oceanographic Data Center.[7] Malcolm Rigby was concerned with much of this work.

Benbow has reported on a system at the Boreal Institute for Northern Studies, University of Alberta, Canada, which he claims to be the first fully-integrated on-line system for a UDC library.[10] It uses *Universal decimal classification for use in polar libraries*, produced by the Scott Polar Research Institute, Cambridge, England, and allows searching by author, title, subject, UDC number and accession number. The hierarchical and faceted features of UDC were found to be particularly convenient for the searching and thesaurus construction.

Another on-line interactive system is operational at the Water Resources Data Systems Document Reference Centre (WATDOC) of Environment Canada.[11] Here a UDC Water Thesaurus Concordance links a special water vocabulary with a subset of the UDC water schedules. The machine readable form of the schedules and concordance eases updating, ensures the currency of the thesaurus/concordance and allows savings in time and cost. The universal nature of UDC is particularly useful for the bilingual data base, which includes French language input.

Conclusion

Major advantages of UDC are its flexibility, the hierarchical notation, and the specificity which it allows. This specificity is considered a major factor at the British Institute of Management and at ICI Fibres, but it is only achieved at the expense of long and complex notations. On the other hand the comment was made at the University of Bradford that the long notations of Dewey can present greater filing problems than those posed by UDC. The University of Bath and the British Institute of Management show that it is possible to amend UDC to suit the needs of an individual library and to simplify the notation. It is also possible to use a simpler notation on the shelves than in the classified catalogue, albeit at the risk of greater confusion to readers.

The British Library Working Party on Classification and Indexing found that in 1973 UDC was being used by twenty-two per cent of all British libraries but for only five per cent of all library holdings, the difference being presumably because it is mainly special libraries, with very specialized holdings, which use UDC.[12]

Doubts have been expressed about the future of UDC, partly because of its slow revision process and its dependence on an out-dated structure as originally set forth in Dewey. The trend from UDC to DC in Norway was noted in chapter one, which also includes comments on why one British university (City University) has changed from UDC to DC. On the other hand, UDC appears to lend itself to mechanization and this must be a very real point in its favour.

Work linking UDC with a new SRC (variously called Standard Reference Code, Standard Roof Code or Subject-Field Reference Code) as part of the UNISIST Broad System of Ordering (BSO) is still in the experimental stage, so a detailed account would be out of place in a book concerned with classification and indexing *practice*. Foskett's thorough survey of the past, present and future of UDC gives information about this development.[13]

References
1 Porter, R T 'The library classification of geography' *Geographical journal* 130(1) March 1964, 109-112.
2 van Helm, Joh 'Use of UDC in a mechanized system: its application in a KWIC program' *Special libraries* 63(10) October 1972, 482-486.
3 Kien, Joh P H G 'Relating the Library of Congress subject headings to UDC in the framework of the PICA project' *Open* 3(9) September 1971, 553-557.
4 Personal communication from Joh P H G Kien.
5 Barnholdt, B 'A computer-based system for production of a UDC-classed library catalog at the Technological University Library of Denmark' *Libri* 18(3-4) 1968, 191-196.
6 Barnholdt, B 'The computerization of the UDC-classed library catalogue of Danmarks Tekniske Bibliotek, Copenhagen' *Libri* 21(1-3) 1971, 234-245.
7 Rigby, Malcolm *Computers and the UDC: a decade of progress 1968-1973.* The Hague, International Federation for Documentation (FID), 1974. (FID 523).
8 *op cit*, 72-73.
9 Freeman, R R *Research project for the evaluation of the UDC as the indexing language for a mechanized reference retrieval system: an introduction* New York, American Institute of Physics, 1965 (AIP/DRP UDC-1); Freeman, R R *Research project for the evaluation of the UDC as the indexing language for a mechanized reference retrieval system: progress report for the period July 1 1965—January 21 1966* New York, American Institute of Physics, 1966 (AIP/DRP UDC-2); Freeman, R R *Modern approaches to the management of a classification* New York, American Institute of Physics, 1966 (AIP/UDC-3) (also published in *Journal of documentation,* 23(4) December 1967, 304-320 as 'The management of a classification scheme: modern approaches exemplified by the UDC project of the American Institute of Physics'; Russell, M and Freeman, R R *Computer-aided indexing of a scientific abstracts journal by the UDC with UNIDEK: a case study* New York, American Institute of Physics, 1967 (AIP/UDC-4); Freeman, R R and Atherton, P *File organization and search strategy using the Universal Decimal Classification in mechanized*

reference retrieval systems New York, American Institute of Physics, 1967 (AIP/UDC-5) (also published in Samuelson, K *Mechanized information storage, retrieval and dissemination: proceedings of the FID/IFIP Joint Conference, Rome, June 14-17 1967* Amsterdam, North-Holland Publishing Company, 1968, 122-152); Freeman, R R *Evaluation of the retrieval of metallurgical document references using the Universal Decimal Classification in a computer-based system* New York, American Institute of Physics, 1968 (AIP/UDC-6); Freeman, R R and Atherton, P *AUDACIOUS: an experiment with an on-line, interactive reference retrieval system using the Universal Decimal Classification as the index language in the field of nuclear science* New York, American Institute of Physics, 1968 (AIP/UDC-7); Atherton, P, King, D W and Freeman, R R *Evaluation of the retrieval of nuclear science document references using the Universal Decimal Classification in a computer-based system* New York, American Institute of Physics, 1968 (AIP/UDC-8); Freeman, R R and Atherton, P *Final report of the research project for the evaluation of the UDC as the indexing language for a mechanized reference retrieval system* New York, American Institute of Physics, 1968 (AIP/UDC-9). Also published in 'Seminar on UDC in a mechanized retrieval system', Copenhagen, September 1968, *Proceedings*, edited by R Mölgaard-Hansen and Malcolm Rigby. Copenhagen, Danish Centre for Documentation, 1969 (FID/CR report no 9).

10 Benbow, J A 'On-line automation of a UDC-based library' (in American Society for Information Science, Western Canada Chapter, fourth annual meeting, Winnipeg, Sept 28-29 1972 *Proceedings*, edited by Anne B Piternick. Vancouver, British Columbia University, School of Librarianship, 1972. pp 113-121).

11 McCuaig, Helen E and Mercier, Marcel A 'Use of a thesaurus/classification concordance for indexing and retrieval' (in American Society for Information Science *Proceedings Vol 10. Innovative developments in information systems: their benefits and costs*, edited by Helen J Waldron and F Raymond Long. Washington, ASIS and Westport (Conn), Greenwood Press, 1973. (Thirty-sixth annual meeting, Los Angeles, Calif, Oct 21-25, 1973). pp 129-130).

12 British Library Working Party on Classification and Indexing *Final report* Boston Spa, British Library, 1975. (British Library Research and Development Report no 5233). p 13, para 26.

13   Foskett, A C *The Universal decimal classification: the history, present status and future prospects of a large general classification scheme* London, Bingley, 1973.

For further information about UDC see Foskett chapter eighteen, Maltby/Sayers chapter ten, and G A Lloyd in Maltby pages 99-118.

Chapter Three

THE LIBRARY OF CONGRESS CLASSIFICATION

THE LIBRARY OF CONGRESS CLASSIFICATION (LC) dates from the beginning of this century and was compiled following the decision of Herbert Putnam, after the library had moved to a new building in 1897, that there should be a new scheme devised specifically for its collections. The result is a series of special classifications, each with its own index, reflecting the literary warrant and subject departmentalization of the Library of Congress. This emphasis on published literature was a major reason for the admiration of the scheme by two distinguished British librarians of the first half of the twentieth century, Wyndham Hulme[1] and Savage.[2]

Although the first volume (E-F: American history) was published in 1901, it was not until the 1970s that the scheme was completed with the publication of class K, Law. LC has not published a general index to the scheme, but two indexes were published by other organizations in 1974.[3,4] Revised editions of individual classes are published infrequently, but the scheme does undergo continuous revision (mainly in the form of additions and expansions) and details are given in the quarterly *LC classification: additions and changes*. These additions and changes are cumulated by the Gale Research Company of Detroit, Michigan.

When studying LC it is important to remember that it was intended for one library only, that of the US Congress. It has, however, been widely adopted by other libraries, especially academic libraries.

An excellent account of the history of the scheme has been provided by La Montagne.[5] More recently there have been valuable studies by Philip Immroth, who devoted a considerable amount of time to studying and explaining the scheme before his untimely death in 1976.[6-8]

LC in the United States and Canada

Immroth reports that LC is used by a majority of US academic and research libraries as well as some major public libraries, but does not quote figures.[7] Of the libraries in the ten per cent sample investigated by Comaromi, Michael and Bloom, 133 (14.6 per cent) were using LC compared with 779 (85.4 per cent) using Dewey.[9] Of those libraries containing 500,000 volumes or more, however, 114 (62.3 per cent) were using LC compared with sixty-nine (37.7 per cent) using Dewey. These 114 libraries comprised 103 university libraries. Clearly LC is in the ascendency in the larger academic libraries in North America and the literature has revealed a trend towards the scheme in recent years. An analysis by Mowery[10] showed that 159 college and university libraries changed from DC to LC during the period 1968-1971 and three libraries changed from some other scheme to LC. The following are the figures quoted by Mowery for the use of DC and LC in 1160 college and university libraries in 1967 and 1971:

	1967		1971	
	No	%	No	%
LC	473	40.8	635	54.7
	(111 of which had changed from DC)			
DC	588	50.7	429	37.0

Two of the many libraries which have reported their reasons for re-classifying from DC to LC are those of Western Kentucky University[11] and Arkansas State University.[12]

The library of Western Kentucky University decided in 1971 that DC was inadequate for its needs, and LC was chosen for a number of reasons. a) It was preferred by many faculty members; b) it was favoured by librarians, who considered that it is advantageous for large collections and also makes for speedy and accurate processing and therefore greater economy; c) it would make the use of MARC tapes more feasible; d) it would facilitate bibliographic searching since users would be able to go straight from the *National union catalog* to the shelves; and e) professional staff would be freed to work on books not catalogued by the Library of Congress.

Arkansas State University chose to reclassify in 1966 because of the advantages of employing LC proof sheets in card reproduction and also because of a conviction—which proved to be correct—that there would be increased use of LC in academic libraries in the 1970s.

Although dated now, the proceedings of an American Library Association Institute on the use of LC contain very useful information on attitudes of US libraries to LC, problems in various classes and assignment of author numbers, and reasons for and methods of re-classification.[13] Maurice Tauber, summarizing the views of eighty-one libraries (forty-one university, thirty-five college, three public and two state) on LC, states that problems include lack of guidance in the schedules, infrequent changes of subject headings and difficulty in keeping track of changes in the classification.[14] Two frequently cited problems which have now been partially solved were the lack of a general index and the need for a schedule for Law (class K). Fifty-five libraries had changed to LC, most of them from DC but two from Cutter's Expansive Classification. Of these, nineteen said that their arrears had decreased since changing to LC. Asked whether they found it difficult to apply machine methods to LC notations for preparing book catalogues or processing, forty-seven said not applicable yet, twelve said no and three yes.

In the final paper at the institute, Phyllis Richmond outlined the advantages and disadvantages of using LC.[15] Advantages include its ability to cope with vast areas of knowledge; its essentially practical and functional nature and the fact that it was designed for books; an ordinal notation which is helpful as a shelving device; its use on LC cards and MARC tapes; and the quarterly *LC additions and changes*, which allow class numbers to be changed 'relatively painlessly'. Disadvantages include the lack of an instruction manual for its application; the fact that there is no logical order; and the diffuseness or relative nature of the scheme, which can particularly be a disadvantage in a small library. It was also somewhat grudgingly admitted that the non-hierarchical notation can be a disadvantage for enquiry work.

LC in Britain

LC is much less popular in Britain, according to a survey undertaken by the Library Association Research Department in 1972: of 940 libraries returning questionnaires, only thirty-six were using LC.[16] These figures are not completely accurate since seventy-six libraries did not return questionnaires and other sources show, for example, that the National Library of Medicine Classification and the London Classification of Business Studies are much more popular than this survey indicates (see chapter six). Even so there is little reason to doubt that LC is, as indicated by the survey, a poor third to DC and UDC. In fact the British Library Working Party on Classification and Indexing found that in 1973 LC was only being used by two per cent of all British libraries and applied to six per cent of the country's library holdings.[17]

Case studies are given below of three British libraries which use LC (one university, one public and one special) and another library which did use it until 1974.

University of Liverpool

Most of the stock of the University of Liverpool's libraries is classified by LC. The main exceptions are the engineering science stock in the Harold Cohen Library (the main science/medicine/engineering science library) and the books in the architecture library, both classified by UDC, and the music library, classified by a modified version of the British Catalogue of Music Classification (see page 119).

LC numbers given in the *National union catalog* (NUC) are used as a guide when classifying, but for various reasons it is not always possible to accept NUC notations as they stand. First there is the problem of trying to achieve consistency because of the many examples of 'dual provision' in LC. LC is, of course, a series of special classes, each devised for a particular department of the Library of Congress, and there seems to be little machinery for co-ordination between these departments. For example, Military antiquities appears at Greek and Roman antiquities (DE61.M5), Greek antiquities (DF89) and Roman antiquities (DG89) as well as under Military science (U750-856), while Education in the classical world is at DF85 (under Ancient Greece), DG85 (under Ancient Rome) and LA71-81 (under Education).

Secondly there is the problem of delay in receiving notations for new subjects which means that the university often has to make its own decisions which may conflict with official LC notations.

Thirdly a number of amendments were made in the Arts Reading Room, the only department of the library which has always attempted to use LC in a conventional manner, and these have been continued, partly because of the excessive labour which would have been involved in reclassifying and partly because the amendments make better provision for British needs. For example LC makes no provision for 'general' regions of Britain such as North and South, so the following subdivisions appear at HC257 (Economic history and conditions—Great Britain) and DA670 (Great Britain—history and topography, by region):

.A4 North of England
.A41   North-east
.A42   North-west
.A5 South
.A51   South-east
.A52   South-west
.A6 Midlands

Also, the following amendments are made when LC specifies alphabetical division by country, in order to allow for more specific classification and a more suitable sequence under Great Britain.

1 For the basic instruction 'divide by country A-Z', Britain is interpreted thus:

Britain (General) or England G7
Scotland   G71
Ireland   G72
Wales   G73

giving

Trade associations of Great Britain HD2429.G7
Trade associations of Ireland   HD2429.G71

| Trade associations of Ireland | HD2429.G72 |
| Trade associations of Wales | HD2429.G73 |

2 When the instruction 'divide by country A-Z' has two subdivisions—'under each 1) general works, 2) local works A-Z'—the same interpretation applies, giving:

Cottage industries of Britain	HD2336.G7
Cottage industries of Sussex	HD2336.G7.S
Cottage industries of Scotland	HD2336.G71

3 When the instruction 'divide by country A-Z' has three subdivisions, Britain/England is interpreted thus:

Britain/England	G71-G73
Scotland	G741-G743
Ireland	G751-G753
Wales	G761-G763

giving

Child labour in Britain (documents)	HE6173.G71
Child labour in Britain (general)	HE6173.G72
Child labour in Britain (local)	HE6173.G73
Child labour in Scotland (documents)	HE6173.G741

etc.

4 When the instruction 'divide by country A-Z' has four subdivisions, Britain/England is interpreted thus:

England/Britain	G71-G74
Scotland	G751-G754
Ireland	G761-G764
Wales	G771-G774

giving

Water rights —England (general works)	HD1697.G71
Water rights —England (international aspects)	HD1697.G72
Water rights —England (by region — Sussex)	HD1697.G73.S
Water rights — England (by town — Brighton)	HD1697.G74.B
Water rights — Scotland (by region — Moray)	HD1697.G753.M
Water rights — Scotland (by town — Elgin)	HD1697.G754.B

The University Library is a subscriber to the UK MARC service, but LC numbers on UK MARC tapes are considered even less acceptable than those in NUC.

All the library staff with whom I spoke were able to point to disadvantages in the use of LC, and there was general agreement about these except that one person described class H as 'much more satisfactory than Dewey's treatment of the social sciences' while another thought it 'very bad', pointing to LC's lack of provision for synthesis as one of its chief faults. For example there is a place in class H for Trade unions and race problems (HD6490.R2) and for British trade unions (HD6460) but not for British trade unions and race problems. The books on this subject must therefore be classified either at HD6490.R2, separated from books on British trade unions, or immersed with general studies of British trade unions at HD6460.

An area which is found to be inconsistent and which could again be improved by the use of synthesis is the provision of divisions within British reigns. For example, the following subdivisions are provided for twentieth century England:

DA566   General works
  .2   General special
  .3   Minor works. Pamphlets etc
  .4   Social life and customs. Civilization. Intellectual life
  .5   Military and naval history
  .7   Political and diplomatic history
  .8   Caricature, satire etc
  .9   Biography and memoirs, A-Z

It is not, however, possible to specify political and diplomatic history, social life and customs, or satire under a particular ruler, yet there is a vast amount of literature on, for example, social life and customs under Edward VII and political life under George VI while the reign of Elizabeth II is an important one for satire.

The excessive detail provided for some authors, such as Shakespeare and Goethe, is not considered particularly helpful for undergraduates, who would be happier with a straight alphabetical sequence. This detail is not provided for modern authors, resulting in inconsistency.

The notation is considered too long and complex in many areas and the frequent use of decimal subdivisions after a non-decimal number is considered confusing.

I was glad to hear one of my frequent 'academic' criticisms confirmed by a practising librarian: it is not a good idea to separate regional history and topography of Britain (at DA670) from local history and topography (at DA690), so that Lancashire, for example, appears in DA670 but Lancaster in DA690.

In 1972 staff and students of Liverpool Polytechnic's Department of Library and Information Studies carried out a survey of reactions of users of the university's arts reading room to the LC classification, as part of the UK catalogue use survey organised by the Library Association Cataloguing and Indexing Group. Of 343 students questioned, only 158 (forty-six per cent) found LC helpful for browsing purposes and only 103 (thirty per cent) found it useful for locating books on specific topics. The following were among the comments made:

'scattering of geography unhelpful'
'Dewey Decimal Classification easier'
'arrangement of politics bad'

'too much juxtaposition of unrelated topics'
'numbers too long and complicated—easier to remember figures'
'more specific classification needed'
'the letters and numbers system is quite inferior to other systems'
'confusing to remember three, four or five numbers after letters'

In spite of the obvious problems of LC, as revealed in the staff and student reactions quoted here, the general feeling is that the scheme works quite well and is probably the most satisfactory for the library.

Edinburgh City Libraries

Edinburgh City Libraries is the only British public library system to be classified by LC. The scheme replaced fixed location and closed access when Dr E A Savage became principal librarian in 1922. Readers of Dr Savage's excellent *Manual of book classification and display for public libraries*[2] will be aware of his high opinion of LC in comparison with the Dewey Decimal classification. Surprisingly, however, the junior library was and is classified by a simplified version of DC, partly because of the need for compatibility with libraries maintained by the Department of Education. Perhaps also Dr Savage considered DC easier for children to follow, although the transition from junior to adult library must surely be made more difficult.

One of the problems in introducing LC was that not all classes were published at the time that the library was classified. For this reason Savage produced classifications for Religion (BL) and French literature (PQ) which are unique to Edinburgh. The fact that he did not produce alphabetical indexes for either class did not facilitate matters for the Edinburgh cataloguing staff.

The following table shows the main classes for religion at Edinburgh with equivalents from the official LC tables:

Edinburgh		LC
BL	Religion	BL
540	Mythology	BL 303-325, 660, 700-820, 830-875
880	Non-Christian religions	BL660-2630
BM	Judaism	BM
BR	Christianity	BR
1960	Roman Catholicism	BX801-4793
3660	Protestantism	BX4800-4861
4420	Anglicanism	BX5003-5740
4965	Methodist churches	BX8201-8495
5060	General religious history of Scotland	BR780-789
BS	Bible	BS

Edinburgh		LC
BT	Christian doctrine. Theology	BT
BV	Practical Christianity	BV
BX1	Collected religious writings of Christian authors, A-Z	—
20	Preaching	BV4200-4315
41	Collected sermons	BV4240-4316
50-2575	Sermons by individual preachers	BV4253-4254 (but placing under denominations preferred)

Perhaps learning from this experience, Edinburgh decided not to anticipate the long awaited class K (Law) but simply to class all law books at K and arrange them alphabetically by author. This means that the library is now faced with the task of classifying a large amount of material.

For French literature, Savage had an interesting idea which was later to be adopted by Ranganathan in his Colon Classification: he decided to represent each author by a notation which was the same as the date of their birth followed, if necessary, by the initial letter of their surname. For example:

PQ1000	Authors by date of birth
1802H	Hugo, Victor
1803A	Aubert, Claire
1803D	Dumas, Alexandre (père)
1824B	Boisgobey, Fortune du
1824D	Dumas, Alexandre (fils)

An interesting amendment in the Music Library is the use of MA (unused in LC) for works by and about individual composers instead of scattering the composers according to form or instrument. For example MA407 represents Mozart and the following are extracts from the subdivisions for this composer:

MA407	Mozart
.4	Songs
.5	Piano
.10	Woodwind
.25	Organ
.26	Opera

Another variation is the classification of the history of musical instruments and techniques for playing instruments with collections of music for that instrument and not, as in the official LC, in a separate sequence.

In the Fine Art Library, class N is used with very few amendments apart from necessary expansions. For example several art galleries have had to be inserted in the art galleries sequence, such as

N1219 D67	Doncaster
1263	Dudley
1403	Langham
1404	Leeds

Another area where extensive changes have been made is British topography. The unsatisfactory separation of cities and towns in a particular geographical area from each other and from their county is replaced at Edinburgh by a much more satisfactory geographical arrangement, the following being examples of subdivisions:

DA674	Lancashire
.1	Furness
.6	S.W. Lancashire
.65	Southport
.7	Liverpool and Bootle
.75	Mersey
.8	Wigan
.9	St Helens
DA678	West Midlands
.1	Shropshire
.2	Shrewsbury
.3	Other places, A-Z
.4	Staffordshire
.5	The five towns
.6	Stafford
.7	Burton-upon-Trent

A very interesting special department at Edinburgh is the Scottish Library, containing material on Scottish life and letters. This is really a general-special library, since it houses material on most subjects relating to Scotland other than those appropriate to the subject collections in Music and Fine arts. The notation X, unused in LC, is placed in front of the appropriate subject number for all material in this department, giving for instance:

X L	Scottish education
X TA	Engineering in Scotland

Material on Edinburgh is housed in the Edinburgh Room and given the notation Y followed by the appropriate subject number. Very detailed classification of areas and buildings is made possible by allocating a separate notation to the various squares of a street directory map of Edinburgh.

There are extensive collections of prints and slides in the Edinburgh Room, the Fine Art Library and the Scottish Library and these are successfully classified by LC, with their own indexes. The only other library to house a large amount of non-book material is the Newington Branch Library. The collection of records and cassettes here is arranged in broad subject groups and catalogued by cards issued by various commercial services.

LC was very popular with all members of the Edinburgh staff to whom I spoke, including the subject librarians. The fact that several former members of staff had introduced LC into libraries to which they had moved was also mentioned to me as evidence of its popularity. The main snag in its application is the provision of numbers for new subjects not enumerated in LC but the library is usually successful in choosing an appropriate number. For example, HC240 was chosen by Edinburgh for the European Economic Community and LC chose HC241!

Departments of the Environment and Transport

The library of the Department of the Environment has used LC since 1943 when it was known as the library of the Ministry of Town and Country Planning. In 1970 the Department of the Environment was formed by merging the Ministry of Housing and Local Government (as it had become) with the Ministry of Transport. The latter was using the Universal Decimal Classification system. Following the merger, discussions took place as to whether LC or UDC would be the more suitable scheme to adopt for the new library and it was decided to use LC, one reason being that the LC-classified stock was the larger so that less reclassification would be needed. Much, but not all, of the UDC stock was reclassified (see page 183). In September 1976 the Department of Transport was set up, and the library now provides a service to the two departments, Environment and Transport.

The library contains approximately 250,000 books with accessions at the rate of approximately 250 per week. In addition, author and classified indexes of periodical articles have been provided since 1946.

LC works very well and is generally liked by the library staff— sometimes after an initial revulsion (possibly due to library school teaching). The cataloguing staff are able to judge the scheme's merits and deficiencies as they all spend one day a week on enquiry work.

Disadvantages of the scheme include insufficient detail in some important areas and inadequate treatment of British localities. To cope with these problems special schedules have been developed in some areas including Leisure, recreation and tourism (GV); Transport (HE, TC, TE-TG); British local government (JS); Land use, transportation planning and housing (NAC, an unofficial expansion of NA, Architecture); Pollution (RA); Sanitary and municipal engineering (TD); and Energy (TM). The NAC expansion was based on a scheme devised to cover the needs of the School of Landscape Architecture at Harvard University, unofficially known as the 'Harvard expansion',[18] expanded to emphasize British planning law and practice and particularly the concept of town *and country* planning.

The following examples from these schedules illustrate some of the deviations from standard LC practice and some of the subjects which can only be classified because of the Department of the Environment's own amendments.

D of E   *LC*

GV LEISURE, RECREATION AND TOURISM
    (LC—RECREATION)

1000	Tourism and holidaymaking	G155
		(Tourist trade)
.1	Bibliographies	—
.4	Periodicals	—
.6	Yearbooks. Annuals	—
.8	Dictionaries. Glossaries	—
1001	Organizations. Societies	—
1002	Statistical surveys	—
1003	History	—
1004.4	Application of mathematical techniques	—
.6	Research	
1005.2	Legal aspects	—
.4	Administrative and managerial aspects	—
.6	Labour aspects	—
.8	Economic aspects	—
1006	Social aspects	—
.6	Choice of time for holidays	—
1007	Influence of tourism on planning	—
1008	Education	—
1009	International tourism	—
.1-1019	By place	—
	Touring by car	—
1020	Periodicals	—
1021	General works	—
	By place	—
1022	United Kingdom, A-Z	—
1023	Other countries, A-Z	—
1027	Organizations. Societies	—
	Holidays on inland waterways	—
1030-1037	as 1020-1027	—
1040-1047	Cycling. as 1020-1027	GV1041-1059

65

D of E		*LC*
2660	Footbridges	—
2680	Pedestrian subways	—
2700	Separate roads for pedestrians. Pedestrian segregation generally	—
2760	Moving pavements	—

TF RAILWAY ENGINEERING   TF

4000-5300 AIR CUSHION VEHICLES		—
4000	General works	—
4300	Tracks	—
4400	Buildings	—
4420	Terminals	—
4500	Vehicle design and construction	—

NAC2000-2310 LAND USE. TRANSPORTATION PLANNING

2000-2054	General	—
2047-2054	By place	—
2055-2289	Road transport aspects	—
2076	Parking facilities	—
2155-2163	Relation of streets to buildings	—
2236	Pedestrian precincts	—
2284	Planning of areas under elevated roads	—

RA441-1285 PUBLIC HEALTH. ENVIRONMENTAL HEALTH AND POLLUTION

441-538	By country (LC — Public hygiene exhibitions by country)	
540-559	Noise	RA772.N7
570-578	Air pollution	—
579-590	Other types of pollution	—
1185-1285	Environmental pollution	—
1198	Economic aspects	—
1199	Insurance against pollution	—
1201	Governmental responsibility, including law	—
1215	Research	—
1230-1231	Poisons	—
1260	Food poisoning	—
1280	Pesticides	—
1285	Artificial fertilizers	—

D of E		*LC*
TM ENERGY		—
1-10	Form divisions	—
12	Research	—
14	Statistics	—
16	Legal aspects	—
20	International	—
21-124	By country	—
200-299	Technical aspects	—
300-399	Economic aspects	—
400-599	Political and conservation aspects	—

Another problem area is the management aspects of computers. There is no place for this subject in LC but the Department of the Environment has added the following:

HF5678	Computers
.2	Periodicals
5679	Dictionaries, glossaries etc
.9	Thesauri of computer terms

The need is felt by the cataloguing staff for a fuller expansion.

A list of British place names in Cutter number sequence has been developed, following local government reorganization in 1974, for use wherever geographical subdivision is called for. Some examples are given below. (District councils in capital letters):

A93	Avon
B5	BERWICK-UPON-TWEED, Northumberland
B51	BEVERLEY, Humberside
B512	Bewcastle, Cumbria
B52	Bewdley, Hereford and Worcester
B8	BRISTOL, Avon
K59	Kirkby, Merseyside
S624	SLOUGH, Berkshire

For practical classification the schedules are mounted and filed in loose-leaf form with cross-references to related schedules. A note at the front of the transport schedules is reproduced as figure four.

There is a classified catalogue, which is now being closed and photo-copied in book form following the adoption of the Anglo-American Cataloguing Rules 1967 in January 1977, together with a computerized subject index. This is compiled broadly on chain indexing principles, so that 'distributed relatives' are collected:

LIME	
Agricultural use	S643
Production: chemical technology	TP886
Properties and testing	TA434-435
Soil stabilisation	TA710
Water purification	TD468

RELATED NUMBERS
The following subjects are classified in other parts of the Library of Congress
schedule:
Town and country planning, including transportation studies   NAC
Noise   RA 540-559
Air pollution   RA 570-578
Aircraft. Aeronautical engineering   TL 500-999
Ships. Shipbuilding   VM

NOTES
Indentation is used to indicate the hierarchical structure of these schedules. It is
essential to identify the hierarchy to appreciate the full meaning of a number.
Thus the number HE 5800 which is described as urban transport and is in the road
transport section, is the number for urban road transport. The class numbers
themselves are not hierarchically based, and so are no indication of the schedule's
structure.
Operation of transport services, traffic control and works about vehicles in relation
to one another are classified at HE. The schedules in the T section are for the
vehicles themselves, their tracks and equipment.
The alphabetical index covers most numbers in the schedules, but the general
subdivisions listed at HE 2-18 (and applicable in many other places) and the
country numbers are omitted. Not all the possible combinations suggested in the
schedules by "As . . . " are included. For example, motor vehicle parts are
indexed only where they appear in the schedule at TE 4001-4097. If the index
is used, as it is intended, in conjunction with the schedule, these omissions
should not lead to any difficulties.

Figure 4: Note at beginning of special schedules for transport
Departments of the Environment and Transport Library

Readers are helped to find their way around the library by bay guides (see figure five). Training courses are also organized for new staff.

HC 240 – HD 1410
ECONOMICS. LAND

HC Economic history and social
   conditions (contd)
   240   Europe; EEC
   241-260   Great Britain
   257 (A-Z)   by region or county
   258 (A-Z)   by town or city
HD Economics (specific topics)
   101-1395 Land; real estate
   1380   Property law

Figure 5: Bay guide, Departments of the Environment and Transport Library

---

Wigan Reference Library, Greater Manchester

LC was introduced into the Reference Department of Wigan Public Libraries by A J Hawkes in the late 1920s. The reference library was formed as a result of a bequest of £5000 from a local industrialist, and LC seemed a suitable choice for a scholarly collection which formed a larger reference library than was usual in a town of Wigan's size. Also, Hawkes had used LC in his previous library, the National Library of Wales.

Hawkes made a number of modifications, often transferring emphasis from the USA and North America to Britain and Europe. For example the geographical schedules for class N (Fine arts) were changed as follows to ensure that material on Britain and Europe filed first:

	Table II		Table III		Table III-A	
	LC	Wigan	LC	Wigan	LC	Wigan
America	01	83	01	114	01	137
North America	03	84	03	116	03	139
USA	05	85	05	118	05	141
Canada	29	89	41	131	41	151
Europe	83	2	125	3	125	3
Britain/England	85	4	128	6	128	6
England – local	87	6	131	9	131	9
Scotland	89	8	134	12	134	12

Again, the form divisions of TN (Mineral industries) (TN 1-19) were replaced by revised geographical divisions as follows:

Wigan		*LC*
TN MINERAL INDUSTRIES		TN
0	General	145
	Europe	
1	General	55
2	Britain/England	57
3	English counties, A-Z	58
4	Scotland	61
5	Counties, A-Z	62
6	Wales	63
7	Counties, A-Z	—
8	Ireland	59
9	Counties, A-Z	60
10	Special British companies	—
12	Other European countries, A-Z	65-95
14	America: North America	21-22
15	Canada: British North America	26
16	Provinces	27
17	USA	23
18	States, A-Z	24

Much greater detail was provided for British history and topography, where the schedules were completely rewritten. The countries of Europe, Asia, Africa and Oceania were moved from DC/DZ to E, and America was given only one class (F) instead of the original two (E and F). DC/DZ were used for regions of Britain, thus:

DC	Southern England
DD	Wessex
DE	West Country
DF	Thames and Thames Valley
DG	Eastern England
DH	Norfolk
DJ	Midlands
DK	Northern England
DL	Lancashire
DM	Lake District. Welsh border countries. Cheshire
DN	Wales and Welsh Marches
DQ	South Wales
DR	Isle of Man
DS/DV	Scotland
DX/DZ	Ireland

Various other amendments were made to provide a more helpful collocation or more up-to-date schedules, such as the movement of stamp collecting from HE6187/6230 (under Postal services) to NK9840/9874 ('unofficial' subdivisions, under Fine arts) and the provision of a new place for Aircraft (VZ) following Naval science.

The present chief librarian in the Metropolitan Borough of Wigan, Mr N E Willis, found LC a satisfying scheme to use during the period when he was reference librarian. There was frequently a shorter notation than would have been the case with DC, as well as greater detail and a more logical arrangement. Since DC was used in the Lending Libraries, there was inevitably some confusion for the staff with the use of two schemes, but this confusion was not so great as might have been expected because, until the reorganisation of local government in 1974, Wigan was unusual in that each department and each branch did its own classification and cataloguing.

With the advent of a centralized ordering and cataloguing system and with the formation of the Metropolitan Borough of Wigan, the decision was taken in 1974 to adopt DC for all new intake. This means that the above comments are perhaps out of place in a book dealing with current classification and indexing practice, but they do indicate how a scheme like LC can be adapted to the requirements of a very British library like Wigan.

LC in two other countries

Before describing the modifications to LC introduced by Lagos University, Nigeria, S A Orimoloye surprisingly describes the scheme as 'by far the most popular classification scheme of all',[19] perhaps because it is used by many Nigerian libraries. Modifications at Lagos include a complete restructuring of class DT (African history); the classification of many architecture books at TH (Building) instead of NA; the classification of some scientific material at T (Technology) instead of Q (Science) and vice versa; the classification of most agricultural material at QK (Botany) or QL (Zoology) instead of S (Agriculture) because there is no Agriculture Faculty at Lagos; and the classification of all subject bibliographies with the subject followed by the mnemonic 5 (a strange phenomenon for LC!), so that a bibliography of civil engineering is TA5 instead of Z5851-5854 and a bibliography of history is D5 instead of Z6201-6209. Orimoloye warns against excessive modifications, however, because these mean that the value of standardization is lost and 'undermine the international applicability of LC'. 'With modification', says Orimoloye, 'as with everything else, it is in place to counsel moderation.'

R A Ukoh explains that Ibadan University Library, Nigeria, decided to reclassify from the Bibliographic Classification to LC in 1975, partly because of dissatisfaction with aspects of BC (see page 91) and partly because of three major advantages of LC: its suitability for large research collections; the fact that it is used on LC catalogue cards and MARC tapes; and its use by the other five large libraries in Nigeria as well as the small but growing libraries of the colleges of technology.[20]

The University of Tasmania decided to abandon the Bibliographic Classification in 1973 for reasons which are given on page 91. The choice of scheme lay between DC and LC, and LC was chosen because a) it would allow easier reclassification of older materials by reference to the *National union catalog* and LC printed catalogues; and b) LC numbers are usually call numbers rather than simply class numbers and are thus more effective for retrieval of specific items.[21]

Conclusions

The trend to LC is not unique to the United States, as seen in the examples of Nigeria and Tasmania. One wonders whether LC is sometimes adopted for the wrong reason—the convenience of the library staff rather than helpfulness to the reader. It has to be admitted, however, that reducing cataloguing costs and speeding up the cataloguing process by making use of centralized services is likely to prove beneficial to readers.

In Britain LC is far less popular, but the libraries described in this chapter are generally happy with the scheme, though they have all had to make a number of amendments. Their experiences, however—and that of Wigan Reference Library—show that LC can be very effective for a library which needs detail in the places where LC provides it and is willing and able to make appropriate amendments to the schedules.

References
1 Hulme, E Wyndham 'Principles of book classification' *Library Association record* 13, 1911, 354-358, 389-394, 444-449; 14, 1912, 39-46, 174-181, 216-221. (Reprinted by the Association of Assistant Librarians, 1950, as AAL reprint no 1).
2 Savage, Ernest A *A manual of book classification and display for public libraries* London, Allen & Unwin and the Library Association, 1946.
3 Canadian Library Association *An index to the Library of Congress classification* by J McRee Elrod et al. Preliminary ed Ottawa, Canadian Library Association, 1974.
4 Olsen, Nancy B *Combined indexes to the Library of Congress classification schedules* Washington, US Historical Documents Institute, 1974. 15 vols.
5 LaMontagne, Leo E *American library classification with special reference to the Library of Congress* Hamden (Conn), Shoe String Press, 1961.

6 Immroth, John Philip *A guide to the Library of Congress classification* 2nd ed Littleton (Colorado), Libraries Unlimited, 1971.

7 Immroth, John Philip 'Library of Congress Classification' (in Kent, Allen (ed), *Encyclopedia of library and information science* New York, Marcel Dekker, 1975. Vol. 15, pp 93-200).

8 Immroth, John Philip 'Library of Congress Classification' (in Maltby, pp 81-98).

9 Comaromi, John P, Michael, Mary Ellen, and Bloom, Janet *A survey of the use of the Dewey Decimal Classification in the United States and Canada* Lake Placid Foundation, Forest Press, 1975.

10 Mowery, Robert L 'The "trend to LC" in college and university libraries' *Library resources and technical services* 19(4) fall 1975, 389-397.

11 Wassom, Earl E, Custead, Patricia W, and Chen, Simon P J On-line cataloguing and circulation at Western Kentucky University: an approach to automated instructional resources management *LARC report* 6(1) January 1973. 78pp.

12 Taylor, Gerry M, and Anderson, James F 'It will cost more tomorrow' *Library resources and technical services* 16(1) winter 1972, 82-92.

13 Institute on the Use of the Library of Congress Classification, New York City, 1966. *The use of the Library of Congress Classification* edited by Richard H Schimmelpfeng and C Donald Cook. Chicago, American Library Association, 1968.

14 Tauber, M F 'Review of the use of the Library of Congress Classification' (in ref 13, pp 1-17).

15 Richmond, Phyllis A 'General advantages and disadvantages of using the Library of Congress Classification' (in ref 13, pp 209-220).

16 Sweeney, Russell 'Dewey in Britain' *Catalogue and index* (30) summer 1973, 4-6, 15.

17 British Library Working Party on Classification and Indexing *Final report* Boston Spa, British Library, 1975. (British Library Research and Development report no 5233). p13, para 26.

18 Pray, James Sturgis, and Kimball, Theodora *City planning: a comprehensive analysis of the subject arranged for the classification of books, plans, photographs, notes and other collected material* Cambridge (Mass), Harvard University Press, 1913.

19 Orimoloye, S A 'Lagos University modifications to the Library of Congress Classification' *Nigerian libraries* 8(1) April 1972, 45-50.

20 Ukoh, R A 'Library classification and change: the example of Bliss' *Libri* 25(3) September 1975, 168-173.

21 Goodram, R, Howard, M, and Eaves, D 'The University of Tasmania's reclassification programme: the first year *Australian academic and research libraries* 5(3) September 1974, 101-112.
For additional comments on LC see Foskett, chapter twenty-one, and Maltby-Sayers, chapter eleven.

Chapter Four

THE BIBLIOGRAPHIC CLASSIFICATION

HENRY EVELYN BLISS spent almost half a century perfecting his Bibliographic Classification (BC). The result is perhaps the most interesting of all the general classification schemes but one which appeared much too late to challenge the supremacy of DC, UDC and LC. It also falls between two stools—basically an enumerative scheme, it has many synthetic features with several auxiliary schedules to allow detailed specification under some subjects. A good example is schedule 12, applicable to class G (Zoology), which allows more satisfactory classification under a particular animal than other classification schemes. But it is an irritating scheme to use because of the scattering of the auxiliary schedules, the lack of pagination to help locate them, and the very poor index.

Bliss died only two years after the completion of his scheme, so he was never to know that, although it was never popular in the USA, his own country, his scheme was to be used in several British libraries. The enthusiasm of British users was such that they formed the British Committee for the Bliss Classification, reconstituted in 1967 as the Bliss Classification Association under the lively chairmanship of Jack Mills. For several years Mills has edited the annual *Bliss classification bulletin*, issued originally by the H W Wilson Company and now by the Bliss Classification Association, and issues of this have contained revised classes for some subjects including astronomy, atomic energy and printing. More important, the association initiated a radical revision of BC with Mills as editor, assisted first by Valerie Lang and later by Vanda Broughton. The first three volumes of this were published by Butterworths at the beginning of 1977 (Introduction and auxiliary schedules, class J Education and class P Religion).

Another important development was the publication by the School Library Association in 1967 of the *Abridged Bliss classification*. This is a very useful abridgment which is claimed to contain sufficient detail for sixth form needs and which also contains some revision. For example there is a rearrangement of physics, botany and zoology and there are places for a number of concepts excluded from the original BC such as cybernetics, space travel, teaching machines, econometrics

76

and the European Economic Community. There is also provision for collecting all aspects of geography should libraries wish to do so. Anthony Eare has described the use of the scheme to reclassify the library of Oakham School, Rutland.[1]

The Department of Health and Social Security (DHSS)
The Ministry of Health (now the Department of Health and Social Security) adopted BC in 1948, having previously been classified by Brown's *Subject classification*. BC seemed a natural choice for reclassification, partly because class H (Anthropology and medical sciences) was developed from CC Barnard's *Classification for medical libraries*. It was partly through the influence of the Ministry of Health library that BC was adopted by a number of other health care libraries such as those of some of the National Health Service authorities and of the King Edward's Hospital Fund for London.

The relatively broad classification allowed by the first edition of BC works well for shelf arrangement of books, an alphabetical subject catalogue being used for the retrieval of specific items of information. It was, however, occasionally necessary to expand the schedules, as in the following example at HIU, Industrial hygiene, which had no expansion in the original BC:

HIU Industrial hygiene. Occupational hygiene
- A Industrial health services
- B Environment hygiene of occupation
- D Industrial health surveys
- F Industrial morbidity and mortality. Absenteeism
- H Industrial nutrition
- J Industrial physiology. Posture. Fatigue. Hours of work. Night work
- L Physical examination of employees
- N Industrial psychology (alternative for IWT)
- P Industrial accidents and injuries. Safety devices
- S Industrial toxicology (alternative for HZQI)
- U Industrial dust. Air sampling
- W Noxious occupations, industries, trades, manufacture etc.

Subarrangement on the shelves, unusually but helpfully, is by date of publication, this date being placed underneath the class number to give the shelf mark. Thus, a document entitled *The social aspects of alcohol and alcoholism* by S Cartuana and M O'Hagan, published in 1976 by Edsall for the Medical Council on Alcoholism, is classified at QMA/1976. This subarrangement is also very helpful in stock weeding especially if, as is the case at DHSS, material is automatically considered for withdrawal or for relegation to storage after a fixed shelf-period. At DHSS this period is fifteen years.

Towards the end of 1948 a classified index of periodical articles was started, containing items listed in departmental publications. Current publications include *Hospital abstracts, Current hospital literature, Current literature on health services* and *Social services abstracts*. The schedules did not contain nearly sufficient detail for the precise classification required in this index and in particular could not cope with multi-faceted topics. Sometimes facets of a subject could be indicated by using an existing auxiliary schedule, but frequently the schedules were not detailed enough and it was necessary to combine parts of the same schedule, which Bliss did not allow. Provision was made for this by using a colon to combine concepts within a class, a method which—though different in application—resembles the retroactive notation which is a feature of the revised BC (see pages 81-90). Examples from two expansions showing the use of this device are given below.

Example 1

HIB Health services (part of an expanded schedule designed to provide a framework for the arrangement of current literature on the health service; to provide for more specific classification of items in HIB; and to take account of the reorganization of the National Health Service).

HIB	Health services
K	Staff
KA	Manpower — staffing needs/levels
KC	Personnel management
KD	Recruitment
KE	Conditions of service
KF	Salaries and wages
KG	Superannuation
KH	Others
KK	Training
KM	Welfare
KP	Industrial relations

HIBL	Types of staff
A	Administrative
B	Finance
C	Medical
D	Physicians' assistants, Medical assistants
F	Dentists
J	Nurses
K	Health visitors
M	Midwives
P	Pharmacists

Q	Opticians
S	Scientific and technical staff
U	Paramedical staff
W	Ancillary staff

HIBN	Facilities
A	Design
B	Construction
C	Cost
D	Location
F	Maintenance
J	Types of facility
K	Hospitals
L	Health centres
M	Nursing homes

Multi-faceted topics may be expressed by using the fourth and fifth letters of a classmark (ie those following the base notation HIB) after a colon, so that a document on the training of dentists may be classified at HIBKK:LF and HIBLF:KK and one on the salaries of hospital administrators at HIBKF:LA:NK, HIBLA:NK:KF and HIBNK:LA:KF.

Example 2

QF Social security (a new schedule which replaces QAN-QAP from the original BC)

QF	Social security
A	British social security in general
AB	Actuarial aspects
AG	Abuses
AJ	Selectivity, means tests
AK	Welfare rights
AL	Claims, claimants, claimants' unions
AM	Ideas not yet incorporated
AN	Reverse income tax

QFC	(British) National Insurance scheme
A	Contributions
B	Flat rate
C	Employed persons
D	Self-employed persons
E	Non-employed persons
F	Graduated or earnings-related contributions
H	Benefits
I	Unemployment
J	Sickness and invalidity
JA	Medical certification

JB	Hospital deductions
JC	Constant attendance allowance
K	Maternity allowance and grant
L	Widows' benefits
M	Guardian's allowance
N	Child's special allowance
P	Retirement pension
PA	Graduated
PG	Reductions for earnings
R	Death grant

Again, multi-faceted topics may be specified by adding, after a colon, the letters following the base notation QF. Thus, QFAJ:CL and QFCL:AJ indicate means tests for widows.

There is also a general table of regional and anatomical subdivisions, which may be applied throughout class H after a full stop (thus distinguishing them from the subdivisions of schedule 13 which are applicable after a comma). The following is an extract from this schedule:

A	Head, face and neck
AD	Head
AM	Face
AV	Neck
B	Thorax, chest
C	Abdomen
D	Trunk
E	Peritoneum and serous sacs
F	Superficial fossae
G	Upper and lower extremities, Limbs
H	Skin generally
I	Skins, regional
J	Hair, nails etc
K	Skin glands etc
L	Bones
M	Joints
N	Cartilages, Bursas, Ligaments
O	Muscles, Tendons, Fasciae
P	Respiratory system
PC	Upper respiratory tract
PF	Nose
PG	Nasopharynx
PH	Paranasal sinuses
PJ	Throat
PK	Larynx
PM	Pharynx

PN	Tonsils
PO	Trachea
PP	Bronchi
PR	Bronchioles
PS	Lungs
PT	Pleura
PV	Diaphragm

As an example of the application of this table, HPNN.PS,E represents a document on the cause of lung cancer: HPNN is the original BC notation for cancer, PS (from the above schedule) is lungs and ,E (from the original schedule 13) means causation of disease.

All the expanded schedules at DHSS were developed after an examination of the periodical literature—an excellent example of literary warrant.

Also included in the index to periodical articles are entries for specific titles in series which are shelved together, such as Hospital building notes, Hospital design notes, Hospital building progress reports, Hospital equipment notes, and Local authority building notes. This is a recognition of the fact that a classification scheme developed for the retrieval of specific items of information is not necessarily ideal for shelf arrangement.

It is unlikely that DHSS will reclassify its stock by the revised edition of BC, but it is planning to adopt the new edition for future additions as far as possible. The revised schedules are already being used to construct a thesaurus for information retrieval.

The National Foundation for Educational Research (NFER)

BC was adopted by NFER in the 1950s because of its suitability for education. One of the major problems in its application is the treatment of topics in relation to types of schools (for example, discipline in secondary schools or primary schools as opposed to school discipline in general). This problem is overcome in the second edition by the use of retroactive notation:

	Old BC	Revised BC
Discipline in schools	JHH	JGS
Discipline in primary schools	—	JMG S
Discipline in secondary schools	—	JNG S

NFER has made a number of amendments to the original BC, an example being the following expansion of JKD (Reading):

JKD	Reading
B	Reading machines
C	Secondary and adult reading
D	Basic skills
F	Study skills

I	Reading, language and speech	
J	Special alphabets	
K	Reading disability and remedial reading	
M	Research. Surveys of reading ability	
O	Testing reading ability	
R	Book surveys: all age and ability levels	
S	Book analysis of reading material: word frequency, readability, subject matter, etc	

The hyphen is used where appropriate to indicate phase relationships, as suggested by Bliss. For example, *Progress and problems in moral education* is classified at JKY-PE, JKY being an expansion at the foundation library to mean 'teaching of other subjects' and PE being the original notation for 'ethics and moral conduct'.

University of Lancaster

When the university library was formed in 1963 the decision was made to adopt BC for a number of reasons. The flexibility of BC, with its many alternatives, was attractive in view of the interdisciplinary nature of many of the proposed courses at Lancaster. In addition there was doubt as to whether the Library of Congress and Decimal classifications were appropriate for an academic library, although consideration was given to the use of LC for arts subjects and UDC for science, technology and possibly the social sciences. A home-made scheme was also considered, but time did not permit this.

There have been many amendments to the original BC schedules due partly to academic pressure (before the library became fully established), partly to inadequacies of BC and partly to the special needs of the library.

Among the many examples of minor amendments and expansions are the following from class M (History):

Lancaster		*BC*
MB	Europe	MB
MBL	10th century	—
MBLE	11th century	—
MBLT	12th century	—
MNQ	Soviet Union	MNQ
MNQP	1917-1924	—
MNQQ	1924-1952	—
MNQR	1952-	—

MNZ is used for Finland instead of MN&, thus eliminating the unfortunate use of &, which has no filing significance. In the original BC, MNZ was used for Latvia.

Another minor change is the use of . instead of , to introduce notation from the auxiliary schedules, thus:

MNZ   Finland

MNZ.B   Political history (from schedule 4a)

More substantial changes include the production of detailed new schedules for the Middle East countries because of the existence of an important department of Arabic and Islamic studies, the complete revision of a number of schedules including English language and literature (Y), Librarianship (Z) and Music (V), and the compilation of special schedules for Goethe and Shakespeare.

As is well known, Bliss provided four alternative methods of classifying literature. The Lancaster method is something of a hybrid, the general pattern being

Forms (general history and collections)

Periods

    Forms

    Individual authors

The following extracts from Lancaster's class Y illustrate some of the differences between Lancaster's practices and the original BC:

Lancaster		*BC*
Y	English language and literature	Y
YA	English language	YA
8	English language teaching	YA8
81	Dictionaries	YA81*
82	Bibliographies	YA82*
83	History and geographical treatment	YA83*
86	Textbooks, readers; divided by schedule 2 for textbooks, readers in a specific country	—
869	Textbooks, readers in series; divided by schedule 2 for textbooks, readers in series for use in a particular country	—
YAZ	English language in other countries	—
A	American English	—
B	Canadian English	—
C	Australian English	—
D	New Zealand English	—
E	African English	—
I	Indian subcontinent	—
M	Melanesian (pidgin) English	—
P	Pitcairnese English	—
U	Caribbean English	—
YB	History of English literature	YB

(*Though Bliss would probably not have approved of this use of two numbers from schedule 1)

Lancaster		BC
YBB	History of English poetry	YBB
B	Ballads	YBBB
C	Lyric poetry	YBBC
D	Dramatic poetry	YBBD
E	Epic poetry	YBBE
F	Narrative poetry	YBBF
G	Descriptive and contemplative poetry	YBBG
H	Romantic poetry	YBBH
I	Idyllic poetry	YBBI
J	Limericks	—
K	Carols	—
L	Elegiac poetry	YBBL
M	Pastorals	—
O	Odes	YBBO
S	Sonnets	YBBS
U	Blank verse	YBBU
V	Free verse	YBBV
Y	Other forms	YBBY
YBC	Collections of English poetry (divide like YBB)	YP
YBD	History of English drama and theatre	YBD
YBE	Collections of English drama and plays	YQ
YBF	History of English fiction	YBF
D	Detective stories	—
S	Short stories	—
YBG	Collections of fiction in prose (divide like YBF)	YR
YBH	History of English prose, not fiction	YBH
YBI	Collections of English prose, not fiction	YS
YH	Nineteenth century: history and criticism	YH
YH5	Collections, selections in more than one genre	YH5
YHA	History and criticism	YHA
YHB	Poetry: history and criticism	YHB
YHC	Poetry: collections	YP
YHD	Drama: history and criticism	YHD
YHE	Drama: collections	YQ
YHF	Fiction in prose: history and criticism	YHF

Lancaster		BC
YHG	Fiction in prose: collection	YR
YHH	Prose literature not fiction: history and criticism	YHH
YHHC	Prose literature not fiction: collections	YS

A new subdivision, VZ, is added to class V for music scores, and this section is also used to subdivide VWO, Instrumental history. A feature which would not have been welcomed by Bliss is the use of notational symbols extending to six or eight digits:

VWO	Instrumental history, study and training (divide like VZ)
VZDLAA	Solo violin scores
VWODLAA	History of the violin

Bliss did not provide a filing order for his various symbols but the situation is less complicated at Lancaster because the hyphen and such arbitrary signs as $ and & are not used. The order is 1-9, ., a/z, the following examples being taken from the classified catalogue:

JNR	Secondary education
JNR5	Reports
JNR.MA	Selection procedures
JNR.ME	Examinations
JNReev	Secondary education in Essex

It is strange that the lower case letters, indicating geographical subdivision, should follow rather than precede the more specific subdivisions taken from schedule 14.

Talks with assistant librarians indicated no particular feeling against BC, though I was told that readers occasionally complain about lack of familiarity after being used to Dewey in public libraries and that they also find the mixed notations confusing. The synthetic features were welcomed by at least one librarian.

The assistant librarian in charge of the resource centre feels that BC is no better and no worse than any other classification scheme for non-book materials, the main problem being the physical format of the materials themselves. For this reason alone NBM are not filed in classified order but arranged in accession number order following an arbitrary number indicating the form of media (eg 36 Tape-slide, 26 Cassette). All NBM are, however, included in the classified catalogue; an example of an entry is reproduced at figure six.

Chain indexing is used successfully with the classified catalogue. The following are examples of entries from the computerized subject index:

FILMS: BIBLIOGRAPHY	ZJKD
FILMS: EDUCATION	JIV
FILMS: MUSICAL ACCOMPANIMENT (STUDIES OF)	VWVI

Open University. E262. TV Programme 1.

Language in context. (Language and learning).

Open Univ. 1975.
Videocassette. Philips, b & w, 25 mins.

ISBN 0 X 05054524 9. Educational studies: a second
level course. Associated with block 1 of E262.

Figure 6: Catalogue entry for videocassette, University of Lancaster.
(WAK is BC number for Social aspects of language as communication;
35 indicates videocassette; 19 is accession number for this item.)

FILMS: ORGANIZATION: LIBRARIES   ZNGR
FILMS: PERFORMING ARTS   YXP-YXT
FILMS: SPECIAL LIBRARIES   ZTB.VXP

However satisfactory BC may be, the University of Lancaster considers that its use is unfortunate in view of the inclusion of LC and DC
notations on MARC tapes. Had the rapid development of MARC been
foreseen in 1963, BC would almost certainly not have been used.
The Lancaster staff consider that the scheme (as amended) works
reasonably well but that letter notations are not as memorable as
Arabic numbers and that therefore they make things more difficult for
readers.

The university is unlikely to adopt the revised BC schedules in view
of the immense amount of reclassification which this would involve.
A more likely possibility, if retrospective files could be made available
along the lines of the cassettes produced by the London and South
Eastern Regional Library System (LASER), would be reclassification
by LC.

Zoological Society of London

The Zoological Society of London adopted BC in 1965 when its
library was rebuilt. Previously, fixed location had been used. BC was
chosen because it seemed the most suitable scheme, but a considerable
number of modifications had to be made. To begin with, the initial G
(Bliss's notation for Zoology) was dropped from the notation, since
every item in the library is classified solely for its zoological interest.
Leaving Z free to be used for non-zoological subjects if required, this

gave a base of twenty-five letters divided into A-K subject schedules (these had to be almost completely rewritten as the original schedules were quite inadequate), and L-Y taxonomic schedules (these had to be thoroughly revised and one authority was adopted for the taxonomy of each animal group eg Walker's *Mammals of the world* for mammals, Imms' *General textbook of entomology* for insects, and Landsborough Thomson's *New dictionary of birds* for ornithology. This authority is cited at the head of each section of the schedules to which it refers. As the study of animal taxonomy progresses, it may be necessary to adopt new authorities and so revise the schedules).

The following table shows some extracts from the Zoological Society's schedules together with the notation for each subject from the original BC schedules. Asterisks indicate the appropriate authority for the particular class.

ZS		BC
A	General biology	E
AA	General zoology	G
BA	Animal body in general: anatomy, physiology etc of whole body	GA
CA	Major areas of body	GA
DA	Circulatory system	GEA
E	Development, embryological and post-embryological	GDQ
EA	Embryology	GEO
FA	Nervous system	GF
GA	Ecology	GG
HA	Zoogeography	GH
I	Faunistic works — divided directly by geographical number	GI
J	Palaeontology and evolution	GJ (alternative: preferred with EP)
KA	Genetics	EN
*LB	Protozoology (*Kudo *Protozoology* 4th ed 1960)	GLB
*M	Coelenterata (*Webb and Elgood *Animal classification* 1955)	GM
*N	Acoelomata, Worms (*Grassé *Traité de zoologie* vol 4 1961-65)	GN
*O	Coelomata (*Grassé vol 5)	GO
P	Arthropods	GP
*PC	Crustacea	GPC

87

	(*Waterman *Physiology of crustacea* 1960)	
*Q	Insects	GQ
	(*Imms *General textbook of entomology* 9th ed 1957)	
*R	Arachnida	GR
	(*Savory *Arachnida* 1964)	
*S	Mollusca	GS
	(*Thiele *Handbuch der systematischen Weichtierkunde* 1929-34)	
*T	Echinodermata	GT
	(*Boolootian *Physiology of echinodermata* 1966)	
U	Chordata	GU
*V	Ichthyology	GV
	(*Grassé *Traité de zoologie* vol 13 1958)	
*W	Herpetology: Amphibia and reptiles	GW
	(*Kuhn *Familien der ezenten und fossilen Amphibien und Reptilien* 1961)	
*X	Birds, Ornithology	GX
	(*Landsborough Thomson *New dictionary of birds* 1964)	
*Y	Mammals	GY
	(*Walker *Mammals of the world* 1964)	

Bliss's geographical schedules (schedule 2, a/z) are used with few changes apart from additions. However, because the nylon tape used for marking the notation on the spines of books only permitted upper case letters, geographical divisions are introduced by /. Mammals of Great Britain are therefore classified at Y/E on the shelves and $\frac{Y}{e}$ in the catalogue, with an additional card at $\frac{e}{Y}$. The letter I is used to introduce a geographical division on its own, so that IE represents fauna of Great Britain.

A new schedule, x, was developed for Seas and oceans. The anterior numeral classes and the other auxiliary schedules are not used.

Class numbers from the two main groups of the schedules (A/K and L/Y) may be synthesized by means of a comma, so that Y,FA would mean the nervous system of mammals. The comma files before the oblique stroke and both are followed by direct subdivision indicating species of animal, thus:

Y,CN   Bones of mammals
Y/B   American mammals
YDE   Kangaroos

The librarian, Mr R Fish, reports that there have been few problems in the use of the classification except that the occasional reader finds some difficulty with the use of commas and oblique strokes. 'There seems to be no way round this,' he adds, 'except to be thankful we did not use UDC.'

The following examples, taken at random from the shelves of the Zoological Society library, illustrate the use of the classification. The conventional BC notation is also given, an asterisk denoting that this does not specify the exact topic.

ZS		BC
X,AQ	The practical value of birds	GX,U*
X,CN	Osteology of birds	GX,A*
X/B	Birds of America	GXb
X/E	Popular handbook of British birds	GXe
XFB	The biology of penguins	GXFP
XFT	Emperor penguins	GXFP*
XJL	The buzzard	GXJT
XPS	Budgerigar guide	GXPS*
Y,CN	Catalogue of the bones of mammalia in the collection of the British Museum	GY,A*
Y,AQW	Fur-bearing animals in nature and in commerce	GY,U*
Y,DBA	The cranial arteries of mammals	GY,G*
Y/E	Wild animals in Britain	GYe
Y/OR	The mammals of Arabia	GYor
YD	Life of marsupials	GYD
YDE	Kangaroos	GYDL
YGW	The natural history of the African elephant	GYGU
YJB	Living with deer	GYJA
YKZ	The sheep and its cousins	GYJV
YOB	Mustelidae	GYOB
YPM	The cat	GYPM

The mnemonic value of the notation is clearly seen. CN always means Osteology or Bone whether it appears on its own (applying to zoology in general) or synthesized with X (Birds), W (Reptiles) or Y (Mammals).

In order to achieve notational brevity on the shelves, notations with two or three digits are not normally subdivided. This applies to the shelves, and not to entries in the classified catalogue. 'Sexual behaviour in penguins' is classified at XFC (Penguins) on the shelves but has two catalogue entries at $\frac{XFC}{FXK}$ and $\frac{FXK}{XFC}$, FXK being the notation for breeding behaviour.

Tavistock Joint Library, London
The Tavistock Joint Library, serving the Tavistock Institute of Human Relations and the Tavistock Clinic, was classified by the original edition of BC and reclassification by the revised edition commenced in

January 1976. The revised BC was chosen for two main reasons. First it is an up-to-date, faceted scheme with main class marks which would be familiar to readers from their use of the first edition. Secondly it would be possible to reclassify class by class, removing one class at a time from the shelves.

Until reclassification commenced, there was no subject catalogue of the library. The reclassification project provided the opportunity to produce a classified catalogue (with multiple entry in the case of multi-faceted works) supported by an alphabetical subject index. Indeed one of the conditions of the grant provided by the British Library for the project was that a subject catalogue would eventually be published.

An inevitable problem in classifying a library by an unpublished scheme is that of having to use draft schedules which are not yet in a 'settled' state. Particular use is made at the Tavistock Library of classes I (Psychology), Q (Social welfare) and T (Economics), none of which was published when reclassification commenced.

The greater detail made possible by a fully faceted scheme means that the notations are frequently longer than the 'economic limit' of four digits envisaged by Bliss. Nevertheless there are a fair number of three-letter notations and five or six letters is usually the maximum—though some items have eight or even nine letters. The point was made to me that library staff generally have no objection to long notations because they find it easier to file very specific class numbers than having to subarrange more general class numbers by authors. Users of the library were not (in June 1977) finding any difficulty with longer class marks.

Occasionally notations are shorter than they would otherwise be because a facet is deliberately omitted since it is considered unnecessary for the needs of library users. For example, a document entitled 'An experiment in group counseling with male alcoholic inmates' (University of Southern California, 1952) should strictly be classified at QQR NUJ NTD N, building up the notation retroactively from the elements

QDN   Groupwork,
QJN T   Males,
QNU   Alcoholism,
QQR   Prisoners.

(The space after every third letter has no special significance, being simply an aid for retention and filing.) The Tavistock Joint Library decided that it was unnecessary for the needs of its users to specify 'males', resulting in the notation QQR NUD N, with added entries in the classified catalogue at QDN-QQR-QNU and QNU-QQR-QDN.

It will be seen from this example that the library builds up composite class marks retroactively, as instructed in the scheme, with added entries under individual elements linked with hyphens. The

90

entries in the classified catalogue are supported by the following specific alphabetical subject index entries which ensure that readers will find the document from whatever angle they approach it:

Prisoners: Social welfare QQR
Alcoholism: Social problems QNU
Groupwork: Social work QDN

The needs of users and the cost involved are the factors which determine the depth of classification, and each document is considered on its own merits.

The future of BC

In 1969 Mills stated that BC was used by between eighty and ninety libraries,[2] but this figure must be lower now since there have been a number of reports of libraries rejecting BC, usually in favour of DC or LC.

Ibadan University Library, Nigeria, adopted BC in 1948 but R A Ukoh has reported that it became increasingly difficult to use because of its failure to keep up with modern developments.[3] Classification backlogs built up because of the need to try to find places for subjects not covered by the scheme, and the scheme's extra flexibility also presented problems. The radical nature of the revision was unacceptable and Ukoh stated that it did not deal satisfactorily with many West African subjects. Consequently it was decided to adopt LC from January 1975. In a comment on Ukoh's article, Mills pointed out that the schedules to which Ukoh referred were not finalized but had been sent to Ibadan for reactions; he also defended BC's flexibility and pointed out that provision of alternatives would be extended in the revised edition.[4]

The University of Tasmania adopted BC in 1955 but later became disillusioned for four major reasons: the fact that no centralized cataloguing service includes BC notations on its records; the lack of a central organization for the continuation and updating of BC (the Bliss Classification Association being presumably unacceptable to Tasmania); the number of libraries throughout the world abandoning BC including Bliss's own, the New York City College; and the potential cost benefits in terms of processing time of using a standard classification.[5] Accordingly the University of Tasmania too adopted LC from 1973.

In Britain the trend seems to be from BC to DC. The book *Resources and resource centres*[6] contains several examples of the use of BC in the Regional Resources Centre at Exeter, but the following comment appears on page thirty-six following an explanation that BC was used for the growing nonbook collection of the resources centre because of its use in the Institute of Education Library:

There was some disagreement about this. Teachers suggested that it may have been better to use Dewey so that copies of the item cards could be sent out to schools at the same time as they were entered into the library catalogue. The teachers may well have been correct. In fact the institute's library is to be combined with that of St Luke's College of Education in 1978 and will become a section of the university library. It will then be reclassified by DC.[7] A similar fate is likely for the library of Notre Dame College of Education, Liverpool, following its merger with Christ's College of Education and St Katherine's College, both DC users.

Is there then a future for BC? It works well, with modifications, in a number of libraries, as indicated in the case studies. The revised edition is an exciting prospect and this is already being successfully applied in the Tavistock Joint Library. This library was, however, in urgent need of reclassification and was able to secure financial support to enable it to be done. Other libraries are not likely to be so fortunate, and the University of Lancaster has indicated that a change to LC would be more likely if reclassification took place. It remains to be seen whether the revised edition of BC has, like the first edition, come too late to challenge the big three of classification (DC, LC and UDC), especially as two of these are included on MARC tapes and there seems little prospect of BC being granted this accolade.

References
1 Eare, Anthony J 'Reclassification by Bliss' *School librarian* 23(1) March 1974, 18-22.
2 Mills, J Letter to the editor *Library Association record* 71(7) July 1969, 218.
3 Ukoh, R A 'Library classification and change: the example of Bliss' *Libri* 25(3) September 1975, 168-173.
4 Mills, J 'A comment on the article by R A Ukoh' *Libri* 26(2) June 1976, 156-157.
5 Goodram, R, Howard, M, and Eaves, D 'The University of Tasmania's reclassification programme: the first year' *Australian academic and research libraries* 5(3) September 1974, 101-112.
6 Walton, J and Ruck, J (eds) *Resources and resource centres* London, Ward Lock Educational, 1975.
7 Personal communication from J Ruck
For additional comments on BC see Foskett, chapter nineteen, and Maltby/Sayers, chapter thirteen. On the revised BC see: Mills, J 'The Bibliographic Classification' (in Maltby, pp 25-52); Mills, J 'The new Bliss Classification' *Catalogue and index* (40) spring 1976, 1, 3-6;

Mills, J and Broughton, Vanda *Bliss Bibliographic Classification vol 1: Introduction and auxiliary schedules* London, Butterworths, 1977, pp 11-93.

Chapter Five

THE COLON CLASSIFICATION

UNTIL THE COMPLETION of the revised schedules of the Bibliographic Classification, Ranganathan's Colon Classification (CC) remains
the only general scheme to be based entirely on analytico-synthetic
principles. The first edition was published in 1933 and the sixth in
1960. The seventh edition was promised for 1971 but is still not
published.[1]

Ranganathan listed only *concepts* or *isolates*, which were grouped
into *facets* within each main class. For example class S (Psychology)
has two main facets: the person or entity (termed by Ranganathan
the Personality or P facet) and the problem (termed by Ranganathan
the Energy or E facet). The foci in the P facet—an isolate is called a
focus when grouped within its appropriate facet—include the following:

1	Child
11	New born
12	Toddler
13	Infant
15	Pre-adolescent
2	Adolescent
21	Boy
25	Girl

and the foci for the E facet include:

5	Feeling. Emotion. Affection
51	Pleasantness. Unpleasantness
52	Emotion
521	Laughter
523	Joy
524	Anger
526	Fear
53	Affection. Hatred
55	Love
56	Anxiety
57	Sentiment. Interest

The notation for a focus from the P facet is placed directly after
the appropriate class number (though in the seventh edition it will be

94

introduced by a comma) and the notation for a focus from the E facet is introduced by a colon. Thus a book on anxiety is classified at S:56 and one on anxiety in adolescent girls is classified at S25:56.

Until the fourth edition all facets were introduced by a colon but the use in the fourth edition (1952) of the now famous PMEST formula to represent the five facets Personality, Matter, Energy, Space and Time, always applied in this same order, led to the use of the following distinctive indicators:

; Matter
: Energy
. Space
’ Time (changed from . in the 1963 reprint of the sixth edition, 1960).

Class 2 (Library science) is one of the few to contain all five facets and the following examples illustrate the use of the indicators:

2;17	Maps in libraries
2:55	Cataloguing in libraries
234.73	University libraries in the USA
234’N	University libraries in the twentieth century
234;17:55.73’N	Cataloguing maps in university libraries in the USA in the twentieth century

Another interesting feature of CC is the provision for *phase relationship*, or the interaction of one main class (or part of a main class) on another. All phases are introduced by 0 (to be changed to & in the seventh edition) and the particular phase is indicated by a lower-case letter as follows:

a General relation
b Bias
c Comparison
d Difference
g Influence

The following examples illustrate the use of these phase relators to link Science (class A) and Religion (class Q):

AOaQ	Science and religion
QObA	Religion for scientists (ie *biased towards* science)
AOcQ	A comparison of science and religion
AOdQ	The difference between science and religion
QOgA	The influence of science on religion (ie religion *influenced by* science)

According to Gopinath, CC is used in approximately 2500 Indian libraries of many kinds and a few libraries outside India such as the College of Agriculture Library, Khartoum, Sudan.[2] It is not thought to be used in any American libraries or by any British libraries apart from the two dealt with here.

Christ's College, University of Cambridge

Information about Christ's College's use of CC is taken from a guide published in 1970.[3] A major reason for the adoption of CC for post-1800 books was the strong oriental collection housed in the library.

Both alternatives suggested by Ranganathan are used: 2 for 'Mother country' (England) instead of 56 and— for 'Home language' (English) instead of 111, so that England and English file in front of other countries and other languages.

The guide provides a very clear explanation of CC for users of the library, as can be seen from the following extract:

Most of the main classes have their own SPECIAL DIVISIONS, with appropriate symbols; and there may be one or more sets of these special divisions subordinate to one another. Thus in class E (Chemistry), the first set of special divisions is based on the *substance* dealt with and the second set is based on *methods* and *aspects*. Arabic numerals are used for these special divisions. Example: A book on qualitative inorganic analysis would be classed E1:3. E = Chemistry, 1 = Inorganic substances, :3 = Analytical.

Several examples of class marks are given in the guide, including the following:

History of English criminal law Z2, 5v (Z=Law, 2=England, 5= Crime, v=History)

Milton's collected works O—,1K08:x (O=Literature, —=English, 1=Poetry, K08=1608, the date of Milton's birth, x=Collected works)

Origin of species G:6 (G=Biology, 6=Genetics)

The French Revolution V53L (V=History, 53=France,L=18th century)

Metal Box Limited, London

The fourth edition of CC was adopted by Metal Box Limited in the 1950s for a number of reasons. The Universal Decimal Classification, which is used in the Company's Engineering Library at Boreham Wood, did not at that time have any expanded schedules for a number of subjects of special importance to the company such as packaging, food technology and printing. Also there were considerable attractions in the flexibility and specificity offered by a fully faceted scheme.

Very few amendments were made to the scheme but there were a number of major expansions such as Industrial safety and health (D91), Plastics technology (F52), Food technology (F53), Printing technology (M14) and Packaging (M98). Some of the expanded schedules were seen and approved by Ranganathan. The expansion for Packaging appears below:

96

M[P]
97   LEATHER INDUSTRY
98   PACKAGING
  M98 [P], [2P]; [M]: [E]
FOCI IN [P]
1   Metallic containers
11   Cans
12   Aerosols, Pressurized containers
2   Non-metallic containers
21   Boxes, cartons
22   Bottles, Phials, Squeeze bottles
23   Jars
24   Cases
3   Flexible packaging
31   Bags
32   Tubes
33   Sachets
34   Films
FOCI IN [2P]
1   Seams, Joints
2   Bodies, Cylinders
3   Labels
4   Closures
41   Ends, Lids
411   Stoppers, Caps
5   Necks
6   Dispensers, Valves
7   Tapes, Sealing bands
8   Surfaces
FOCI IN [M]
1   Metals
11   Tinplate
12   Blackplate
13   Aluminium
131   Aluminium foil
2   Rubber
4   Plastics, Plastic foams; subdivide as F52[P]
5   Laminates
6   Glass
8   Paperboard, Cartonboard
9   Wood
FOCI IN [E]
1   General packaging methods
11   Gas packaging

111	Nitrogen
113	Carbon dioxide
12	Vacuum packaging
13	Aseptic packaging
2	Design
21	Decoration
3	Manufacture
31	Forming, Tooling
32	Closing
33	Lacquering, Coating
34	Laminating
35	Printing
36	Proofing
37	Cleaning
371	Sterilizing
4	Testing, Inspection
41	Law, Regulations, Standards
5	Labelling
6	Storage
7	Spoilage
71	Corrosion
72	Mould
73	Odour
8	Transport

The scheme in use now is a combination of the fourth, fifth and sixth editions of CC together with Metal Box's own schedules, which are always used as the first authority before the sixth edition is consulted.

A more recent adaptation has been the discarding of the five phases recognised by Ranganathan and the use of the colon followed by the subject device for all phase relationships. For example, *Scientific research in British universities and colleges* is classified at A:2y5:(T4:2) instead of A:2y50bT4:2. (A:2y5 is an example of a Metal Box expansion meaning research projects lists; there is no expansion at all of class A (Science) in the sixth edition of CC). This use of the colon to express all phase relationships is interesting in view of the usual argument that CC provides greater precision than UDC in expressing phase relationships.

The staff at Metal Box are generally satisfied with CC, the only problem being the occasionally complicated notation. 'Occasionally' is stressed since, as will be seen from the appendix, many class numbers are very brief. It needs to be borne in mind, however, that CC is only used for books (approximately 15,000 in all). Reports, pamphlets and similar items are arranged numerically, subject retrieval being via an alphabetical subject list again using faceted principles (see pages 152-4).

The complicated notation does raise occasional problems for staff and users and could also create difficulties in a computer-produced catalogue. Mainly for the latter reason a change to UDC in all libraries is under consideration, though it is recognised that this would probably mean that some special subject interests of the library would not be so well catered for.

A classified catalogue is maintained, supported by a chain index. The following is a brief extract from this index:

FOOD: AGRICULTURE J3
FOOD: ALUMINIUM: METALLURGY F1231:(F53)
FOOD: ANALYSIS E:4:(F53)
FOOD: BIOCHEMISTRY E9:(F53)
FOOD: BRAND NAMES: DIRECTORY F53n.k2
FOOD: CANS: PACKAGING M9811:(F53)
FOOD: INSECTS K86:(F53)
FOOD: LABELS: CANS: PACKAGING M9811:(F53)
FOOD: SELF-SERVICE: STORES: ECONOMICS X525:(F53)

Conclusion

Interesting though CC is, it is used very little outside its native India, and hence this chapter is the shortest in this book. One practical problem of CC is unevenness of coverage—some of the technologies are given scanty treatment for example, which is why the Metal Box Company had to make its own expansions. Some expansions have been published in issues of *Library science with a slant to documentation*.

Complex notation is another obvious problem, though it could be argued that CC's notation is not much more complicated than that of UDC. The difference is that UDC uses only figures whereas CC accompanies its auxiliary signs with every kind of ordinal notation—upper and lower case letters, figures and even Greek letters.

The Metal Box Company uses the fourth edition of CC supplemented by later editions. Maltby/Sayers points out that Christ's College, Cambridge, also uses the fourth edition and is often unable to accommodate changes in later editions.[4] In other words the changes introduced in successive editions of CC do present problems in practice, in spite of Gopinath's assertion that these changes are few compared with the large scale changes taking place in DC.[2] The *changes* may be few but they often involve wholesale reclassification: for example the change of the time indicator from . to ' and of the phase indicator from 0 to & can involve a great deal of alteration to catalogue records and the spines of books.

Although the Metal Box Company considers that the continued use of CC could present complications in a computer-produced catalogue, Gopinath has reported the development by the Documentation Research and Training Centre, Bangalore, of a program for computerized retrieval using CC.[2]

Finally Gopinath states that 'many libraries comment favourably and say that CC gives them autonomy to classify new subjects quickly and consistently.'[2]

References

1 Ranganathan, S R 'Colon Classification edition 7 (1971): a preview' *Library science with a slant to documentation* 6(3) September 1969, 193-242.
2 Gopinath, M A 'Colon Clasification' (in Maltby, pp 51-80).
3 Christ's College, University of Cambridge. Library *A guide to the use of Christ's College library* 1970.
4 Maltby/Sayers, p202.

For additional comments on CC see Foskett, chapter twenty, Maltby/Sayers chapter twelve, and Batty, C D *An introduction to Colon Classification*. London, Bingley, 1966.

Chapter Six

SPECIAL CLASSIFICATION SCHEMES

COMMENTING IN 1969 on the results of classification research, Maurice Line and Philip Bryant said 'virtually all this effort has been theoretical. Some schemes (eg Foskett's London Education Classification) have appeared, but the impact on *library* classification has been small.'[1] If this were completely true, the present chapter would be out of place in a book on classification and indexing *practice*, but the fact is that special classification schemes have been developed to meet practical needs.

A special classification scheme may mean a 'general' scheme designed for a particular purpose or, more usually, a scheme designed for the classification of documents within a particular subject area. In this chapter the use of one 'general-special' scheme and eight specific subject classification schemes is examined. Most of the special schemes show the influence of Ranganathan's faceted approach.

The Cheltenham Classification

An interesting British classification scheme compiled specifically for school libraries is the Cheltenham Classification,[2] used in the library of Cheltenham Ladies' College since its opening in 1894. The first edition was published in 1937. There have been several changes during the eighteen years since the publication of the second edition, and these will ultimately be incorporated in a third edition, which may be available by 1978.

Cheltenham Ladies' College was founded in 1853 to provide an education on Christian lines based on the religious teaching of the Church of England. The curriculum covers a wide range of subjects including divinity, all aspects of arts and sciences, classics, various foreign languages, domestic science, gymnastics and games. The main library contains approximately 20,000 volumes and there is a separate junior library for the lower college (eleven to thirteen age group), an upper college library and subject libraries for English history, classics, modern languages and sciences.

The classification has to be, therefore, a very general scheme, and it is also a very broad one, as can be seen from the following example:

L51	Geography
.22	England
.221	Gloucestershire
.225	Other counties
.226	London

Although Britain's capital city may resent being placed last, it is reasonable that the college's own county should be given precedence!

The classification is sufficiently detailed for the stock which it has to organize and it is also a simple scheme to use. This has enormous advantages, as the librarian (Mrs Mary Harries) points out, in encouraging the students to use the library. It is indeed interesting to note that the college was possibly the first school to begin a library training class, in 1909.

Geography, mentioned above, is one of the subjects which has been reclassified since 1958, having originally been at class P. Other subjects which have been moved and restructured include Science (moved from M to L), Fine arts (moved from S to N) and Education (moved from C60 to C31).

One interesting change in these days of women's lib is the use of C56, a previously vacant number in the Sociology class, for Woman's position. Titles classified here include *The English housewife in the seventeenth century, Votes for women, A London girl of the 'eighties, Women's two roles: home and work, English women in life and letters* and *Women in modern adventure*. In the second edition, Position of women was placed in the Science class at M82.2, under Marriage.

Representatives of more than seventy school and college libraries have visited Cheltenham Ladies' College with a view to adopting the classification. However, only five of the twenty-eight schools which replied to a letter sent by this writer to forty schools in 1976 were using Cheltenham, while an additional four had changed from Cheltenham to Dewey. The following comments were made about Cheltenham:
'I would prefer the Dewey system but only because it appears to dominate. Changing over would involve months of pretty pointless work.'
'The larger the library grows, the less satisfactory its simple classification becomes. Primary pupils coming here, often very well trained in using the local libraries and their own school ones, inevitably have a set-back when faced with a different system. With sufficient time and help, I would most certainly change to Dewey.'
'The scheme seems to work quite well. The main problem seems to stem from the fact that at some time in the past heads of subject departments have been asked to adapt the scheme to their own needs. As this was done independently of each other the result was rather haphazard. What seems to some a simplification (reducing the number

of subdivisions) can make books hard to classify. Heads of department also changed the notation and this has given rise to inconsistency. I believe the result is worse than the original scheme.'

'Pressure from advisers forced a change to a highly simplified Dewey. I personally was quite happy with our modified Cheltenham system. I think it suits a school library admirably, certainly up to about 15,000 volumes.'

'My limited experience of the two systems (Dewey and Cheltenham) so far would suggest that each has its merits and defects. Cheltenham seems a little too general for a library of our size, especially in the science section.'

One school library which still uses Cheltenham is Croham Hurst School, South Croydon, an independent school for girls founded at the end of the nineteenth century. There are no members of staff present now who know the reason for its adoption but it was probably because of its use in Cheltenham Ladies' College. In 1977 the school had 501 pupils, and there are approximately 7000 books in the main library, together with additional collections in the sixth form library, the science library and the junior school.

Although the present librarian is happy with Cheltenham, she would probably have adopted Dewey had she been given the opportunity because of its use in most other school libraries and in the local public library. Most members of the teaching staff are satisfied with the scheme, though the French staff do not like the chronological arrangement of literature and would prefer a straight alphabetical author sequence. The pupils accept the classification critically, even to the extent of occasionally querying class marks; they are probably helped by a 'library period' during the first year in the main school during which the scheme is explained to them.

A number of additions are made to the scheme and, since Croham Hurst adopted the first edition of 1938, some of these conflict with the second edition. The following examples are from the second edition and the Croham Hurst additions are italicized.

C SOCIOLOGY
   III   POLITICAL SCIENCE
      11   Foreign and international relations. Diplomacy. NATO. *The European Community*
   IV   ECONOMICS
      30   Economic history (used by Croham Hurst for *Advertising*, which is logical since C29 is Business methods and Accounting. Advertising is indexed to C29 in the second edition of Cheltenham but this is not indicated in the schedules)

V   SOCIAL SERVICES
  45   Work with young people. Clubs, Scouts, Guides etc. *Children deprived of normal home life. Disturbed children (including research on)*
  48   *Old people*
  49   *Fire service, Life boats etc*
  54   *Work with drug addicts, 'drop-outs', inebriates. Vagrancy*
  55   *Loneliness*
  56   *Race problems* (indexed to M82, under Ethnology, in the second edition)
  57   *Social history of diet*
  58   *Mental health. Mental abnormality. Mental handicaps*
  59   *Welfare work overseas. VSO*
VI   EDUCATION
  65   Secondary education. *Comprehensives*

  72   *Position of women. Women's suffrage. Women's rights. Practical guides on the law relating to women* (at M82.2 in the second edition but note that Cheltenham Ladies' College now uses C56, as reported on page 102)
M SCIENCE
  III   MATHEMATICS
  20   *School maths project (SMP)* instead of Trigonometry
  23   Electronics. *Computers*
  24   *Popular books*
  .1   *Statistics*
  IV   PHYSICS
  27   Practical and experimental. *Technology* (classified at R in the second edition)
  V   CHEMISTRY
  43   Practical and experimental
  .1   *Photography* (R21 in the second edition)
  .2   *Cosmetics*
  .3   *Dyes and dyeing* (R35 in the second edition)
  IX   MAN
  81   Physical anthropology. General
  .1   Prehistoric
  .2   Modern. *Survival. Environment* (indexed to M53, Evolution and heredity, in the second edition). *Pollution. Population (see also P16)*
P GEOLOGY AND GEOGRAPHY
  II   GEOGRAPHY
  16   Migration. Movements of peoples. *Population. Food supply. Conservation. World problems (see also M81)*

Class R (Applied science, Technology) is not used as it is preferred to classify technologies with science.

The small library in the junior school is used mainly by children in the age range nine to eleven. This library was unclassified until autumn 1975, when the librarian decided to adopt Cheltenham in line with the main library although she would have preferred Dewey because the children were used to that scheme in their public library. A colour coding system is used with the classification (for example, green labels on all nature books and red on all histories). The scheme works well in spite of Alasdair Campbell's assertion that it 'would never be suitable for any kind of primary or middle school since it was specifically designed for a secondary school with a dominant academic sixth form and that is still the kind of place where it could most properly be employed.'[3] The main problems are an insufficient breakdown and a complicated notation in places for juniors. For example, much early history is taught to juniors and its treatment in Cheltenham is fairly broad:

D22		Great Britain and Ireland
	.1	Up to Norman Conquest
	.11	Prehistoric
	.12	Celtic Britain
	.13	Roman Britain
	.14	Nordic invasion
	.15	Danish rule
	.16	Saxon and Anglo-Saxon
	.2	Normans
	.1	William I
	.2	William II
	.3	Henry I
	.4	Stephen

The following areas are also considered too broad:

M		SCIENCE
	VII	ZOOLOGY
	74	Lower vertebrates
	.1	Fishes
	.2	Amphibia and reptiles
	.3	Birds
	75	Mammals

Mammals, in particular, needs greater subdivision.

Campbell considers that 'the order and emphasis' of Cheltenham's classes 'are in some ways even stranger than Dewey's' and that 'the minimum requirements for a new edition must include some structural changes, a major expansion of several undeveloped classes, and an alphabetical index altogether more responsive to modern needs'[3], but nine years earlier an American writer, J P Rash, had said, 'the

Cheltenham scheme . . . is a bit weak in philosophy and psychology, but there is no other reason why it should not prove satisfactory for junior colleges or small college collections.'[4]

National Library of Medicine Classification

The National Library of Medicine Classification (NLM)[5] was, as its name implies, designed for use in the National Library of Medicine in Bethesda, Maryland. The preliminary edition was published in 1948. It is an enumerative scheme, very similar in many ways (including notation) to the Library of Congress Classification and it is indeed supplemented by LC at Bethesda and in many other libraries. The similarity between NLM and LC, both in structure and notation, can be seen from the following extract from NLM's Nursing schedule:

WY	Nursing
1	Societies
	Collections
5	By several authors
7	By individual authors, A-Z
9	Addresses. Essays. Lectures
11	History
13	Dictionaries. Encyclopedias
16	Nursing as a profession
18	Education. Outlines. Examination questions. Audiovisual aids
19	Schools of nursing
20	Organization and administration of nursing schools
21	Licensure. Registration
22	Directories
29	Placement agencies
31	Statistics. Surveys
32	Laws. Jurisprudence
77	Economics of nursing
85	Nursing ethics
87	Psychology applied to nursing. Psychological aspects of nursing
100	General works on nursing

One difference is the use of some systematic mnemonics in NLM. For example 32 is always Laws, so that WY32 is laws of nursing, QS132 is laws relating to dissection, W32 is laws of the medical profession in general and WA32 is public health laws.

An investigation by Scheerer and Hines of the classification systems used in 941 medical libraries, reported in 1974, showed that 589 of these libraries were using NLM including 391 US libraries, thirteen in Canada and eleven in Britain.[6] Scheerer and Hines sent questionnaires to twenty-five libraries which had changed to NLM since 1959 and the following reasons were given for reclassification: to take advantage of NLM cataloguing services (thirteen libraries); to provide a better shelf arrangement (eleven); because it is easier to use (ten); to take advantage of regional co-operation (three); because of local circumstances (one); for greater currency (one); because of its arrangement of subclasses (one); and because of its dovetailing with LC (one).

Three years before this survey, Kanchana Sophanodorn had visited five medical libraries using NLM—the New York Academy of Medicine, Cornell University Medical Center, the Albert Einstein School of Medicine, Rockefeller University and the State University of New York, Downstate Medical Center.[7] One interesting finding was that Rockefeller University makes use of mnemonic features as instructed in the preliminary edition of 1948 but not in the third edition. Thus it classifies surgical congresses at WO3 (under Surgery), dental congresses at WV3 (under Dentistry) and congresses on orthopedics at WE3 (under Orthopedics) in spite of the instruction in the third edition of NLM that *all* medical congresses should be classified at W3:

W3   Congresses
        Classify here all monographic and serial publications of
        congresses on medicine and related subjects.

Although Scheerer and Hines only found eleven British libraries using NLM, Jenkins reported in 1976 that it is now the most widely used scheme in British medical libraries.[8] It is used by fifty-nine libraries including several large ones such as Edinburgh University's Central Medical Library, St George's Hospital (Hyde Park, London), the Royal Army Medical College (Millbank, London), Nottingham University's Medical Library, and the University of Southampton's Wessex Medical Library (WML).[9] In parallel with its adoption by WML, it is used in a simplified form by all hospital libraries in Wessex.

WML was started in 1969 from an amalgamation of a number of the departmental libraries of the University of Southampton—those for physiology, biochemistry and zoology—together with the biology section of the main stock. There is also a branch library at Southampton General Hospital developed from the Postgraduate Medical Centre library.

Bearing in mind that the main university library used the Library of Congress Classification, there appeared to be three possibilities for classifying WML: to use LC, to use NLM, or to use some other scheme with a notation adapted for use with LC. NLM was chosen for a number of reasons: first, it was developed in the context of an active medical library and is officially revised fairly regularly; secondly, its structure—stressing organs and systems of the body and specific diseases rather than the traditional disciplines of anatomy, physiology, medicine surgery, etc—reflects the pattern of teaching taking place in the medical school and accommodates more readily the increasingly interdisciplinary literature; thirdly, it fits in well with LC.

For psychology WML uses a special classification developed by the librarian, Mr T A King, when he was at Nottingham University. Based on the subject headings of *Psychological abstracts*, this is placed at QQ and replaces most of BF in the original LC schedules, which is out of date not only in its collocation of Psychology with Philosophy but also in its structure.

The following is the outline of the schedules used at WML, reflecting a combination of LC, NLM, and the special schedule for psychology. The LC classes are italicized.

A	*Generalia*
B	*Philosophy and theology*
C-F	*History and archaeology*
G	*Geography and anthropology*
H	*Social sciences*
J	*Politics and international affairs*
K	*Law*
L	*Education*
M	*Music*
N	*Fine arts*
P	*Language and literature*
Q	*Science*, including
QQ	Psychology
QS	Human anatomy (general works only)
QT	Physiology (general works only) and Biophysics
QU	Biochemistry
QV	Pharmacology and Toxicology
QW	Microbiology
QX	Parasitology
QY	Clinical pathology
QZ	Pathology including Cancer
S	*Agriculture and applied biology*
T	*Engineering and applied sciences*
U	*Military sciences*
V	*Naval sciences*
W	Medicine
601-925	
	Forensic medicine and Dentistry
WA	Public health
WB	Practice of medicine
WC	Infectious diseases
WD100-175	Deficiency diseases

200-226	Metabolic diseases
300-375	Diseases of allergy
400-430	Animal poisoning
500-530	Plant poisoning
600-650	Diseases caused by physical agents
700-758	Aviation and space medicine
WE-WL	Systems of the body (including anatomy, physiology, pathology of the systems)
WE	Musculo-skeletal system
WF	Respiratory system
WG	Cardiovascular system
WH	Haemic and Lymphatic system
WI	Gastrointestinal system
WJ	Urogenital system
WK	Endocrine system
WL	Nervous system
WM	Psychiatry
WN	Radiology
WO	Surgery (including Anaesthesia)
WP	Gynaecology
WQ	Obstetrics
WR	Dermatology
WS	Paediatrics
WT	Geriatrics
WU	Dentistry
WV	Ear, nose and throat
WW	Ophthalmology
WX	Hospitals
WY	Nursing
WZ	History of medicine
Z	*Librarianship and bibliography*

Although NLM is a fairly broad classification, the librarian of WML is not concerned about this as he regards classification as primarily a device for shelf arrangement and prefers to use the alphabetical subject catalogue for information retrieval. Problem areas include disability, underprivilege and rehabilitation. NLM provides the following places for Disability:

W925   Medico-legal aspects of occupational disease and injury (to which the index refers for Disability compensation)

WV32   Otorhinolaryngology: Laws. Estimation of disability for compensation

WW32   Ophthalmology: Laws. Estimation of disability for compensation

W100   Medical service plans: General works (to which the index
               refers for Disability insurance)

Under Rehabilitation, the index refers only to LC schedules UB and UH (Rehabilitation of disabled veterans). There is no entry in the index for Underprivileged.

User reaction after reclassification of WML resulted in the publication of a pamphlet explaining the classification.[10] Since then there has been little feedback, and users appear to accept the scheme.

Science Reference Library Classification

An interesting unpublished British classification scheme is that used in the British Library (Science Reference Library) in London (SRL).

SRL was developed from a scheme developed for the Patent Office library, whose librarian, E Wyndham Hulme, wrote a memorable series of articles in 1911-12.[11] Hulme argued that a classification scheme must be based on *literary warrant*—ie it should concentrate on the way subjects are treated in the literature: if there are books on flame and combustion there must be a place in the schedules for Flame and combustion and not just for the specific subjects; also the classification scheme should not provide excessive detail by enumerating subjects which are not dealt with in the literature held in the library.

A problem with Hulme's application of his theory was that major steps of division were occasionally missed because there was no literature on the more general subject when the scheme was prepared. For example the following subdivisions were provided at TH Fish and fisheries, marine and general:

TH   Fish and fisheries, marine and general
   10   Seals
   11   Whales
   16   Turtles

There was, however, no provision for Sea mammals (of which seals and whales are examples) or Marine reptiles (of which turtles are examples.)

Quite apart from omissions such as this, it is obvious that a scheme developed for the Patent Office in the first quarter of the twentieth century would not be suitable for a major reference library covering the whole of science and technology in the second half of the same century. Mr A Sandison led a team which began revising Wyndham Hulme's scheme in 1963, and he has described the result in a paper given to an FID symposium in November 1976.[12]   The scheme is envisaged as an aid to retrieval, by browsing at the open shelf, of those facts in the literature which escaped the nets of the indexing and abstracting services.

Like the original Wyndham Hulme classification, the revised scheme is an enumerative one. It is under continuous revision in that further subdivisions are provided when classes become overcrowded—a modern application of the literary warrant principle, which is illustrated by the following extracts from the April 1967 and October 1974 schedules for Birds:

	April 1967	October 1974
GC70	Birds, by geographical region	Birds, by geographical region
711	Tropical birds	Tropical birds
713	Temperate birds	Temperate birds
714	Arctic birds	Arctic birds
720	British birds	British birds
7208		Catalogues, check-lists
721		By habitat (eg marsh, woodland types, etc)
722		By other aspects
724	of England and Wales	of England and Wales
7250	of Southwest England	of Southwest England
7251	of Southern England	of Southern England
7253	of Eastern England	of Eastern England
7254	of the Midlands	of the Midlands
7256	of Northern England	of Northern England
726	of Wales	of Wales
727	of Scotland	of Scotland
728	of Ireland	of Ireland
73	European birds	European birds, general, by Taxonomy
730		European birds, general, by other aspects
731		Birds of Northern Europe
7311		of Iceland; of Faeroes
7312		of Norway
7314		of Finland; of Lapland
7316		of Sweden
7318		of Denmark

Similarly classes are deleted if it is found that the literature does not justify subdivisions originally provided, as in the following example:

	1967	*Later amendment*
SF	Fluid mechanics	Fluid mechanics
10	Economics and organizations	Economics and organizations
11	Economic aspects	
12	Research: adminis-tration of, organ-ization of	
130	Corporate organi-zations	
131	Types of organizations	
14	Individual organizations, A-Z	Individual organizations, A-Z

A major principle of the SRL classification is the intermingling of sciences and associated technologies, as seen from the following extract:

CP 00	Botany
DL 00	Agriculture
EP 00	Zoology
GP 00	Medicine
HD 00	Pharmacology
HP 00	Food industries
JB 00	Chemistry
LQ 00	Chemical engineering
LT 00	Chemical industries
NH 00	Mining industries
NV 00	Earth sciences
OT 00	Astronomy
P 00	Mathematics
PQ 00	Physics
PT 00	Nuclear physics
PW 00	Nuclear technology
QJ 00	Radiations
QQ 00	Photography
QV 00	Electricity and electrical engineering

A second, important principle, linked with the first, is *ribboning*, which derives from Wyndham Hulme's idea of a 'chain' of related subjects:

Group will merge insensibly into group—no group containing the entire literature of its subject and each group comprising some proportion of matter foreign to its original definition. . . The unity is that of a chain, not that of a logical system.[13]

The term 'ribboning' is preferred now, rather than chain, in order to avoid confusion with chain indexing. The following extract illustrates the principle at a finer level of detail:

LH 50		Chemical kinetics
LK 25		Effects of physical factors on chemical reactions
26		of pressure
32		of temperature
36		of radiations; photosensitizing of reactions
48		of other variables; of other conditions
5		Other general aspects of chemical kinetics
70		Photochemistry
72		Action of incident light on chemicals
86		Generation of light by chemicals
89		Other aspects of photochemistry
LL 00		Flame, Combustion, Explosions and Explosives
06		Flame and combustion

Other classifications have used similar concepts to the 'ribboning' or 'chain' idea, Bliss's principle of collocation being an example. In marked contrast is the idea that it does not matter where a subject is classed so long as it is indexed correctly—ie that relationships between subjects do not matter.

Other features of the SRL classification include:

1 The classification of books under their inherent subject matter rather than intended audience (eg books on statistical analysis for doctors or for engineers or for farmers are all classified at statistical analysis rather than medicine, engineering or agriculture. This is, of course, an application of Ranganathan's bias phase (statistical analysis *biased towards* doctors etc). It is argued that a) one would *expect* to find a book on statistical analysis under statistical analysis and not at medicine, and b) a problem on statistical analysis can be new to the doctor or farmer but not to the statistician—if there is no book on statistical analysis in farming, a book on statistical analysis in some other application may solve the problem: the book written for the doctor may also help the vet!

2 Frequent use of 'other' classes to allow for unforeseen topics, eg

GC 20		Bird biology
21		Bird behaviour
22		Bird watching
23		Reproductive behaviour
27		Communication
29		Social behaviour
32		Migration of birds

        36   Other special aspects: of bird biology; of bird
                  behaviour
3 'Other' is also used frequently for miscellaneous minor topics not
justifying special classes of their own, eg
    GC 59   Birds: by habitat, general
        60   Ocean birds; Sea birds
        62   Birds of other habitats: general
    This device avoids mixing very specific works on particular habitats
in the generic class, which is reserved for works on a range of habitats.
4 The use of simple notation for an open access library, which is what
the Holborn branch of SRL is (though the Bayswater branch is not
because of the unsuitability of the present building). This is one reason
for the complete absence of synthesis, even extending to the repetition
of form divisions as in the Library of Congress Classification. However
the same digit is used for form divisions wherever literary warrant
justifies enumeration of such divisions, thus providing a mnemonic
element in the notation:
    GC 10   Birds
       113   Encyclopedias
       114   Glossaries; Dictionaries
       115   Abstracts
       116   Bibliographies
    SF   Fluid mechanics
        03   Encyclopedias
        04   Glossaries; Dictionaries
        05   Abstracts
        06   Bibliographies
5 Separation of books, periodicals and microform publications by
using a mnemonic symbol *in front of* the class mark, eg
    (B)GC10   A book on birds
    (P)GC10   A periodical on birds
    (MP)GC10   A microform on birds
    The classification schedules contain many scope notes and cross-
references to other parts of the schedules, for example:
FLUID MECHANICS   (ie the forces exerted on or by a fluid or fluids
                   at rest or in motion, and the movements of the
                   fluid resulting from such forces, including
                   works on liquids or gases treated together or
                   separately.
                       Place here works on the mechanics of the
                   fluid state and/or the mechanical properties
                   of fluids. In general the practical applications,
                   with or without basic theory, are placed with
                   the application.
                            114

Place here works on the forces exerted between a fluid and a solid surface in contact with it. When the work also includes treatment of the utilization of those forces by particular structures, or includes other than mechanical interactions between fluid and surface, prefer placing by the type of structure.

Thus the fluid dynamics of aircraft wings go in 'aeronautics, VB75' and of turbine vanes and rotors in 'Turbines. UH65').

cf Fluids: general . . . . KY 85
      Mechanics, general. . . . . SC 0

for Hydrometry . . . . see PJ 70
      Vector analysis . . . . see PB 82
      Aerodynamics applied to flight . see VB 43
      Vibrations and waves . . . . .see QH 0
      Plasma physics . . . . see QW 6
      Hydraulic engineering. . . . . . . .see VU 0

It is recognized that the classification schedules are only available to the library staff. In the belief that readers need even more guidance than do classifiers, and that they often search *up* as well as *down* hierarchies, cross-references are also provided in the classified catalogue, on guide cards in the catalogue drawers for pre-1973 acquisitions and with the class headings on the microfiches for post-1973 acquisitions, for example:

VQ 46   SHIP DESIGN
        See also:
          Design, general   SW 40-69
          Vehicle design, general   UU 66
          For tank testing of ships SEE VQ 62

On average there are 2.4 references per class and they occur at seventy-five per cent of classes.

Another interesting feature of the classified catalogue fiches is that the title precedes the author in the entry and arrangement within class numbers is in inverted chronological order, on the grounds that readers are more likely to be looking for the most recent material.

Readers are further helped to use the scheme by an alphabetical index to occupied classes and to understand it by the provision of two *Aids to readers*, one entitled *A note on the SRL classification used at the Bayswater branch* and the other *Exploiting subject catalogues at the Bayswater division.*

British Catalogue of Music Classification

The British Catalogue of Music Classification (BCM)[14] was developed not for library use but for the arrangement of entries in *The British catalogue of music*. It is a faceted scheme, arranged in two parallel sequences: musical literature (at class A) and music scores and parts (at classes B-Z).

Among several interesting features of BCM are two relating specifically to notation. First the retroactive principle, whereby any later piece of notation can be qualified by an earlier piece, thus:

DK   Anthems
F   Choral works for female voices
FDK   Anthems for female voices

Secondly the use of a completely non-hierarchical notation, so that a subdivision not only need not have a longer notation than its superordinate term but may even have a shorter one:

PW   Keyboard instruments
Q   Piano
R   Organ
RW   String instruments
RX   Bowed string instruments
S   Violin

A non-hierarchical notation can be a disadvantage in enquiry work (see for example one of the advantages claimed by the British Institute of Management for UDC on page 46) but it can enable a short notation to be used when there is a large amount of literature to be classified on a particular subject and it also increases the scheme's hospitality in array—a new subject can be inserted anywhere even if it is made to *look* subordinate to a co-ordinate subject.

Retroactive notation is a major feature of the revised edition of the Bibliographic Classification (see pages 81, 90), and non-hierarchical notation has always been a feature of BC.

BCM was, as stated, not intended for library use and it has not been widely adopted in libraries. Maureen Long reported in 1972 that only three of 377 public libraries which she surveyed were using BCM, only two of 124 academic libraries and only one of eighteen special libraries.[15] One reason for its unpopularity is undoubtedly its rather cumbersome notation, which can be accepted in a bibliography more easily than for the arrangement of books on the shelves. Another is the problem of reclassification, since the scheme was not published until 1960.

However a number of libraries do make use of BCM, including Craigie College of Education, Ayr (for shelf arrangement of printed music but not for books about music), the National Library of Scotland, Birmingham Public Libraries, Birmingham Polytechnic and (in a much modified form) the University of Liverpool Library.

Until 1957 the National Library of Scotland catalogued music received under legal deposit selectively. In 1957, when BCM commenced publication, this formed the basis of both the catalogue and the classification. Music received under legal deposit is now arranged by the year of acquisition or publication—subarranged by the BCM classification. For the catalogue, BCM is xeroxed twice on cards, once for the composer catalogue and once for the classified catalogue. There is no subject index of the stock, reliance being placed on the subject index of BCM itself.

The following are examples of shelf marks:

Thiman, Eric. Improvisation on hymn tunes. 1957
R/ABZ
(Organ music/exercises in improvisation)

Handel, George Frederick. Two duetti da camera arranged for two treble recorders and keyboard by Ronald Finch. 1962
VSSNTQK/JNE
(VSS=treble recorder; NT=trios; Q=piano; K=arrangements; /JNE= from duets)

Rodgers, Richard. It's a grand night for singing (from the film 'State Fair': piano solo arranged by Louis C Singer). 1959
QPK/DW/JR
(QP=piano solo; K=arrangement; /DW=from songs; /JR=from film music)

Music not received under legal deposit—ie purchases and donations—is catalogued by the British Museum rules and not classified. There is an alphabetical subject catalogue of selected categories of instrumental music, arranged by names of instrument and instrumental combinations.

Until the formation of a separate music department in 1970, the music stock of Birmingham Public Libraries was scattered in several libraries with no fewer than eight different catalogues. A decision was made to close these catalogues and start again, and the opportunity was taken to introduce a more suitable classification scheme than Dewey. BCM seemed the obvious choice and, through the good offices of the BCM staff, the Birmingham music library staff were able to obtain expansions of the original BCM schedules to which further additions have been made as appropriate. The following are examples of these expansions:

Birmingham		Original
AB/AX	Works on music for particular media	AB/AX
AT	Plucked string instruments	AT
ATJR	Lyre guitar	—
ATQ	Harp	ATQ
ATQS	Irish harp	ATQS
ATQT	Autoharp	—

Birmingham		Original
B	Books on individual composers	B
BHQ	Honegger, Arthur, 1892-1955	BHQ
BHS	Howells, Hubert, 1892-	–
P	Music for individual instruments and instrumental keyboards	P
PW	Keyboard instruments	PW
PX	Stringed keyboard instruments	–
T	Plucked string instruments	T
TJR	Lyre guitar	–
TQ	Harp	TQ

A classified catalogue, arranged by BCM, was therefore begun in 1970, though the stock was shelved by a simplified version of DC18 because the BCM notation was considered too complex for shelving purposes and the task of re-labelling the spines of about 45,000 volumes would have been overwhelming.

In 1972 the Music and Sound Recordings Subgroup of the Birmingham Libraries Co-operative Mechanisation Project (BLCMP) was formed, and an agreement was reached to add BCM notations to the catalogue records for printed music and music monographs of all co-operating libraries whether or not the libraries intended to use BCM either in their catalogues or for shelf arrangement. The first classified union catalogue arranged by BCM appeared on microfilm in April 1977. There is as yet no subject index to this catalogue because it is planned to use PRECIS and experiments are still under way.

Two fields were added to the BLCMP MARC format with the approval of the British Library MARC Office: field 085 for the BCM notation and field 089 for verbal feature headings.

One of the co-operating libraries, that of the Birmingham School of Music (now part of Birmingham Polytechnic), adopted a similar system to that of Birmingham Public Libraries—ie arranging its stock by a simplified version of DC and its classified catalogue by BCM—in 1975. Previsouly its books on music had been arranged by the McColvin and Reeves classification[16] and its printed music by a home-made scheme. It is ultimately planned to reclassify the whole library but this is being done at a leisurely pace, particularly in view of the impending nineteenth edition of DC, the music schedule of which is expected to be based on BCM.

The classifiers at Birmingham Public Libraries music library and the Birmingham School of Music are agreed that BCM is a far more satisfactory scheme to use than DC because of the greater specificity which it allows and the ease with which it can be used.

Until 1966 the University of Liverpool's Music Library was arranged alphabetically by composer, making it very difficult to retrieve music by subject, form or instrument. In 1966 it was decided to adopt BCM, considerably simplified in order to make it more suitable for shelf arrangement and with a modified notation.

The main simplification was a reduction in the amount of synthesis used, since complete synthesis was considered unnecessary for a comparatively small collection of 16,000 volumes. The main adjustment to the notation was the use of figures as standard mnemonic subdivisions. For example at N (Chamber music) we find:

N10 Chamber music in general: small orchestra: string orchestra
  30 Trios
  50 Quintets
  60 Sextets
  70 Septets
  80 Octets
  90 Nonets

and these subdivisions may be repeated as required, thus:

NRX   Music for strings alone
  30   Trios

Similarly, under 'Music for individual instruments' we find

10 Solo
15 One instrument, two players
20 Two instruments, two players

giving

PW   Keyboard instruments
  10   Solo
  15   One instrument, two players
  20   Two instruments, two players
RW   Stringed instruments
S   Violin
  10   Violin solos
  20   Violin duets

Although this modified version of BCM works satisfactorily, the librarian would probably choose LC today, in order to achieve consistency with the rest of the University Library.

Thesaurofacet

Thesaurofacet: a thesaurus and faceted classification for engineering and related topics[17] was developed from the English Electric Company's *Faceted classification for engineering*, the first edition of which was published in 1958. It is, however, a completely different work in many ways, not least in its coverage. One of the disadvantages of the original scheme was too great a restriction to the products of the English

Electric group of companies. Thesaurofacet covers the whole field of science and technology but subjects are treated in varying depth and only engineering and allied fields are covered exhaustively.

There is also much more enumeration or pre-co-ordination in Thesaurofacet than in the original scheme, as can be seen from the following examples of class marks from Thesaurofacet and the third edition of the earlier scheme:

	Third ed	*Thesaurofacet*
Aerials	Cm	NO
Circuits	G	L
Receivers	Ck	NV
Television	Cag	NH
Television aerials	Cag Cm	NSN
Television circuits	Cag G	NJA
Television receivers	Cag Ck	NVU

There is still, however, a great deal of synthesis, usually resembling the 'add to' device of Dewey:

V3   Coal technology

      By products

V3B   Coal

V3C   Anthracite

V3E   Bituminous coal

V3N   Coke

      By processes:

      Combine notation from chemical engineering processes with notation for products, for example:

      V3B/UH   Coal processing

      V3C/UH   Anthracite processing

      V3N/UH   Coking

Synthesis can indeed be used wherever required, there being no preferred combination order unless there is an instruction in the schedules. Thus, work study in railway engineering may be either R5/ZGC or ZGC/R5, where R5 represents railway engineering and ZGC is work study.

The most interesting part of Thesaurofacet, however, is the index which acts not only as an index to the schedules but also, in combination with the schedules, as a thesaurus for post-co-ordinate indexing. The following is an entry from the index:

Coatings TYA

RT   Coating

        Preservatives

NT(A)   Enamels

        Lacquers

        Paints

Varnishes
Veneers
BT(A)   Corrosion protection
Materials by purpose

By referring to the schedules at TYA it will be seen that a broader term is Finishing (TU) and narrower terms are Anti-reflective coatings (TYC), Heat resistant coatings (TYD) and Decorative coatings (TYF). *Additional* narrower terms, not classified at TY, are Enamels (VGV), Lacquers (VGS), Paint (VF2), Varnishes (VGL) and Veneers (VGY). Additional broader terms are Corrosion protection (FQ) and Materials by purpose (HX). Related terms are Coating (TU2) and Preservatives (HXM).

The former English Electric Group central library (now the library of GEC Power Engineering, Whetstone, near Leicester) uses the notations in Thesaurofacet for entries in a classified catalogue but continues to use the original English Electric classification for shelf arrangement.[18]

In 1976 the present writer sent circular letters to fifty purchasers of Thesaurofacet in an effort to obtain information about the extent and manner of its use. Of the thirty-six replying, two use it for shelf arrangement, three (these and GEC Power Engineering) use it for pre-co-ordinate indexing by notation—ie a classified catalogue, and four use it for post-co-ordinate indexing by keywords. Sixteen of the libraries make no use of it at all and eight use it for reference, as a guide to thesaurus construction or as a check on indexing terms. Five of the libraries/information centres had closed by 1976. The following were among the comments made about Thesaurofacet:

'We use this scheme only for post-co-ordinate indexing arranged by keyword. For a short time the library book stock was also classified by the scheme using the notation for arrangement, but this did not prove acceptable to the library users.'

'We purchased Thesaurofacet . . . to study it as an aid in expanding the EJC Thesaurus[19] which we used in our first post-co-ordinate (optical coincidence) index. In practice I did not use it as often as I expected to but occasionally found it useful in clarifying relationships of terms which I had to add or amend in the EJC. It has also been useful as an example of a faceted classification scheme to show to non-librarians in the organization who have asked for advice on compiling personal indexes of various kinds of data.'

'We use UDC for shelf arrangement of book material. We thought of changing to Thesaurofacet but the problems are too great with limited resources (eg lack of time to do it, the necessity of extending certain parts of the notation to cover special or broader interests etc.)'

'Thesaurofacet was purchased for use in our reference library . . . for use as the library classification scheme for shelf arrangement and pre-co-ordinate indexing. The index was arranged by keywords and notation. When the research and central libraries were merged Thesaurofacet was dropped in favour of UDC used in the central library. This was a choice based on the problems of integration rather than a straight choice between the two schemes. The central library stock was much the larger and time and effort were consequently less altering the smaller research library stock. One other factor was the lack of provision of an amendment service for Thesaurofacet. As a classification scheme for a library of this kind I like it very much . . . What it lacks is a scheme for continued development. I believe various attempts have been made but money and support have been insufficient. A pity!'

One organization using Thesaurofacet for post-co-ordinate indexing is the Technical Help for Exporters service of the British Standards Institution (THE), set up at Hemel Hempstead in 1966 to help UK manufacturers overcome exporting problems created by foreign technical requirements. Widdowson has described THE's information service and drawn attention to the shortcomings of the original subject retrieval system, using optical coincidence cards, due to the inadequacies of the thesaurus which failed to take account of THE's unlimited range of subject interests.[20] When the ten thousandth document was indexed in 1972, meaning the end of the first sequence of 10,000-hole feature cards, the opportunity was taken to revise the indexing system.

Financial constraints precluded mechanization, so a manual system was sought which would be as comprehensive as possible in terms of subject coverage and would provide sufficient control to ensure consistency by the diversity of people doing the indexing. Two of the most comprehensive English-language thesauri, Thesaurofacet and *Thesaurus of engineering and scientific terms*,[19] were compared and it was decided that Thesaurofacet was the more suitable for a number of reasons including coverage, English terminology and a superior hierarchical structure. Various amendments and expansions were made, with the assistance of Jean Aitchison, in such areas as quality assurance, chemistry and other pure sciences, motor vehicles, machinery, boilers and pressure vessels, and construction engineering. The resulting scheme is called internally *THEsaurofacet*.

The use of a unique 'line notation' allows the required degree of subject coverage to be achieved, with scope for logical expansion should the need arise. Double underlining indicates a major term, or the broadest hierarchical term, which is only used if the document is primarily concerned with that subject field. Simple underlining of notation and term indicates a main term which is used to collect relevant minor terms and so broaden the search. Minor terms are indicated by a single underlining of the term only (not the notation). Vertical lines through terms indicate that they are not normally used as indexing terms (unless underlined); instead the minor or major term immediately above them in the hierarchy is indexed. These points are illustrated in figure seven.

Additions are made to the schedules as required, thus:

SM8	Road drainage components
SM8C	Gulley (Road)
SM8E	Gullet (Road)
SM8G	Drain covers (Road)
SM8H	Drain grids (Road)

The feature cards are filed in separate sequences for countries, subjects and form of publication (eg standards, glossaries, government documents) with an additional sequence for engineers' names in order to assist speedy retrieval of items put into the system by a particular engineer. The numbered holes on the feature cards refer to item cards (see figure eight) and the documents are shelved by country and issuing body ('library ref' on the item card). Thus, the example at figure 8 is shelved under 'France/22:13', 22 representing the Centre d'Etudes de Prévention, CEP, Centre for Accident Prevention, and 13 being the number of the particular document.

There are at present 2,130 technical concepts and 364 countries in the thesaurus and approximately 7,000 of the 10,000 holes of the second set of feature cards (ie the set using THEsaurofacet) have been used during the first five years of the system.

London Education Classification

The second edition of the *London Education Classification: a thesaurus/classification of British educational terms* (LEC)[21] shows the influence of Thesaurofacet by acting as a faceted classification (much more truly faceted than Thesaurofacet) and as a thesaurus for post-co-ordinate indexing. Unlike Thesaurofacet, however, the index/ thesaurus of LEC repeats relationships which are obvious from the schedules, as in the following example:

Economics of education   Ber
- SN Techniques of economic analysis applied to educational systems
- BT Planning of Education
- NT Budget
      Budgetary Control
      Costs of Education
      Financial Resources
- RT Administration of Education

123

SL/SR	CONSTRUCTION ENGINEERING
SL1	CIVIL ENGINEERING

	By process
SL2	Surveying
	*Cartography INW
	*Geophysical and geological measurements YF
	*Surveying instruments XFR
SL3	Chain surveying
SL4	Levelling (surveying)
SL5	Plane table surveying
SL6	Hydrographic surveying
SL7	Soundings
SL8	Underground surveying
SLA	Triangulation
SLB	Curve ranging
SLC	Aerial surveying
SLD	Tacheometry
SLE	Photogrammetry
SLF	Field astronomy
SLFD	Latitude (field astronomy)
SLFF	Longitude (field astronomy)
SLFH	Azimuth determination (field astronomy)

	By civil engineering construction works
	*Water engineering P3
SLK	Demolition works (previously Demolition)
SLL	Blasting
SLN	Earthworks
	*Earth moving equipment T5P
	*Foundations SNO
	*Tunnels SLW
SLO	Excavations
SLO6	Cuttings
SLO8	Trenches
SLOC	Pits
SLOE	Shafts (pits)
SLP	Embankments
SLR	Land Retention works
SLS	Retaining walls
SLT	Drain laying works
SLW	Tunnels
SM3	Road engineering
SM4	Roads
	Subdivide by type
SM4B	Local roads
SM4C	Main roads
SM4E	Motorways
SM4G	Access roads

Figure 7: Extract from THEsaurofacet, British Standards Institution
Technical Help for Exporters, showing unique line notation

Information requested/received (and filed on):

Information requested/received on behalf of:

	Date requested	
	Date answered	

Title & number

CENTRE FOR ACCIDENT PREVENTION
GUIDE TO SAFETY IN DESIGN
AND CONSTRUCTION OF NEW
BUILDINGS

Library ref. FRANCE 22:13	Publication date 1971	Edited
Language	Type & size of doc.	
FRENCH	BOOK	

FEATURES:

FRANCE/WESTERN EUROPE

DOCUMENTS/REPORTS/GOVERNMENT DOCUMENTS/LEGISLATIVE DOCUMENTS/REGULATIONS
(LEGISLATIVE)/NATIONAL
BUILDING/CONSTRUCTION ENGINEERING/STRUCTURAL ENGINEERING/SAFETY
ENGINEERING/HAZARDS/MECHANICAL HANDLING/ELEVATORS/ACOUSTICS/HEATING
ENGINEERING/PUBLIC HEALTH/ORGANISATIONS/ROAD VEHICLE ENGINEERING/
TRANSPORT/CIVIL ENGINEERING/EARTH MOVING EQUIPMENT/MACHINE TOOLS/
INDUSTRIAL SAFETY/ELECTRICAL ENGINEERING/FIRE/TESTING/DANGEROUS MATERIALS,
STORAGE/MATERIALS HANDLING/PEOPLE/BUILDING (TYPES)/APPROVAL
(OFFICIAL)/APPROVAL MARKS/ENVIRONMENTAL DETERIORATION/

see ove

Figure 8: Item card, British Standards Institution Technical Help for Exporters

Economics and Education
Management and Education
Planning

The broader term (Planning of Education, Bep) and the narrower terms (Budget, Bet, Budgetary control, Betb, Costs of education, Betj, and Financial resources, Betm) are all clear from the schedules.

The main facets of LEC, in an order of increasing concreteness, are:

B	Education: foundation, principles, organization
D	Buildings, services, equipment
F	The teaching profession
G	Personnel in education
H	Management of education (Hab-Hrx)
H	Human biology, health and hygiene (Hsb-Hwk)
J	Psychology of education
K	Educand's work
L	Teaching methods
M/P	Curriculum
R/S	Educands and educational institutions
T	Educands with exceptional requirements

The recommended citation order is the reverse of the above schedule order, thus:

Luv	Resource centres
Sav	Polytechnics
Sav Luv	Resource centres in polytechnics

In the first edition the notation for all terms consisted of three letters, the middle one always being a vowel so that the notation was pronounceable with occasionally amusing results:

Pil	Sex education
Ror	Choir school
Ruf	Outward bound schools
Sad	Students in higher education

In order to achieve greater hospitality, the pronounceable element has had to be reduced in the second edition and there are some four-letter notations:

Hsb	Human biology

Mab	Curriculum
Mabb	Curriculum development
Mabd	Curriculum design and planning
Mabf	Curriculum classification

It is partly because of the reduction in the pronounceable element of the notation, which is considered to have a mnemonic value, that Craigie College of Education, Ayr, continues to use the first edition.[22]

126

Neil has suggested that 'it may be that the now very cumbersome notation will act as a deterrent, not only to libraries considering the reclassification of their stock but also to printed bibliographical services which might employ it in the future.'[23]   He regards this as a pity, because 'this new edition is a much better tool than its predecessor.' On the other hand the more cumbersome notation does provide un-limited hospitality, lack of which was one of the chief drawbacks of the first edition.

In the first edition the colon (:) was used to indicate influence and the oblique stroke (/) was used for all other relationships. The University of London Institute of Education now distinguishes five phase relationships, indicated as follows:

:1 General relationship
:2 Bias
:3 Comparison and difference
:4 Influence
:5 Tool

Thus, 'a comparison between internal and external examinations' is Jom:3Jon and 'the influence of punishment on truancy' is Jev:4Jej.

As LEC was devised for the University of London Institute of Education, it is not surprising that it is used in the institute's library. It is, however, only one of about half a dozen home-made classification schemes in use: although there is a considerable improvement in the coverage of such fringe topics as psychology and sociology in the second edition, it is still necessary to retain the other systems which were developed over the years for subjects outside the field of educa-tion.   The general policy is to use LEC as the primary classification scheme for the main lending library and the advanced studies collec-tion and to use it as the first choice for classification if at all possible. Thus, Abraham Maslow's *Motivation and personality* is classified at Jaz (Motivation, in the first edition) even though it is not specifically concerned with motivation in the educational sense, since it is logical to collocate all material on motivation. On the other hand a book dealing in a general manner with local government will not be classified at Bob because it would be misplaced with works on the administration of education.

LEC was adopted for the institute because of the inadequate pro-vision for multi-faceted topics in the former home-made scheme. Owing to the large amount of reclassification which would be involved if a complete change to the second edition took place, classification is still mainly by the first edition supplemented by some expansions from the second edition such as But (Research in education) and Bux (Documen-tation of education).   There are as yet few audio-visual materials in the library, but the intention is to classify these by LEC too whenever possible, to integrate them in the classified catalogue, and to provide additional separate sequences by form of material.

In the classified catalogue multi-faceted works are entered under each facet with the filing symbol underlined, thus:

<u>Maj</u> Jaj Jaz

ACKERMAN, Adrienne
    Dyslexia: motivation
    London: Helen Arkell Dyslexia Centre, 1974
    ii, 13p illus Sbn(pbk) 9503626 1 1

This entry is repeated under Maj <u>Jaj</u> Jaz and under Maj Jaj <u>Jaz</u>, and the following subject index entries are provided on the strip index:

Dyslexia	Maj Jaj
Inability: psychology	Jaj
Motivation: psychology	Jaz
Reading	Maj

Stuart-Jones has commented on some of the disadvantages of the first edition of LEC such as inadequate provision for fringe topics and occasional embarrassment caused by the pronounceable notation.[24] Another problem is that users are sometimes confused by a multi-syllabic class mark after using Dewey and expect to find two or three copies of the book at different class numbers. There is also occasional confusion because of the use of the same term with different meanings, for example 'secondary school' in the sense of both administration of secondary schools and the secondary school curriculum.

As indicated in an article by Stephen Pickles,[25] the thesaurus part of the second edition of LEC is also being used for a computer-produced catalogue of theses and dissertations, covering all theses, dissertations and diploma reports added to the library since September 1975, an extract from which is reproduced as figure nine. The problem of ambiguity caused by the use of the same term in different senses is also found here, and it is considered that 'secondary level' or 'secondary education' would be more appropriate than 'secondary school' when the curriculum is under discussion. It is also found difficult to index some dissertations adequately, especially those from the sociology department (in spite of the expansion of Sociology in LEC2).

However the ease of amendment provided by the hospitable notation complemented by the structured thesaurus makes it quite easy to update LEC in response to new concepts, as shown by the following additions and alterations initiated by the theses and dissertations project:

Bepv   Accountability
        BT   Standards
        SN   Educational accountability in general, both of
                teachers and of school systems

LANGUAGE DEVELOPMENT
HOUSING—PRE-SCHOOL CHILD—BEHAVIOUR—AGE 00-05
RICHARDS CAROL ANN M SC DISS 1971
A SURVEY OF PRE-SCHOOL CHILDREN IN HIGH FLATS: A COMPARATIVE STUDY OF CHILDREN UNDER FIVE AND THEIR
   FAMILIES FROM DIFFERENT HOUSING ACCOMMODATION.
DEPARTMENT OF CHILD DEVELOPMENT AND EDUCATIONAL PSYCHOLOGY

LANGUAGE DEVELOPMENT
IMMIGRANT—COMPENSATORY EDUCATION—ENGLISH AS A FOREIGN LANGUAGE—PRIMARY SCHOOL
                      DUFF MORIA K   M A DISS 1976
COMPENSATORY EDUCATION AND THE YOUNG IMMIGRANT CHILD
DEPARTMENT OF TEACHING ENGLISH AS A FOREIGN LANGUAGE

LANGUAGE DEVELOPMENT
MEMORY—IMMIGRANT—WEST INDIAN—AGE 12-13
MILLWARD IAN   M A DISS 1975
ORGANISATIONAL PROCESS IN THE FREE RECALL OF IMMIGRANT AND NON—IMMIGRANT CHILDREN
DEPARTMENT OF CHILD DEVELOPMENT AND EDUCATIONAL PSYCHOLOGY

LANGUAGE DEVELOPMENT
READING—REMEDIAL TEACHING—INFANT SCHOOL—AGE 05-07
WOLFENDALE SHEILA M SC DISS 1974
THE EFFECTS OF A SHORT LANGUAGE INTERVENTION PROGRAMME WITH INFANT SCHOOL CHILDREN.
DEPARTMENT OF CHILD DEVELOPMENT AND EDUCATIONAL PSYCHOLOGY

LANGUAGE DEVELOPMENT
STORY TELLING—SPOKEN LANGUAGE—AGE 03-07
HARRISON CATHERINE G   M A DISS 1975
FUNCTION AND ORGANISATION IN THE NARRATIVES OF YOUNG CHILDREN
ENGLISH DEPARTMENT

Figure 9: Extract from the University of London Institute of Education's catalogue of theses and dissertations, using the LEC thesaurus for subject headings

(in LEC2 Bepv is 'Standards' without a scope note; the term 'Accountability' is not there)

Jbfd   Language style
        BT   Psycholinguistics
        SN   This term has been added to index the concepts of dialect, slang, 'code' etc, eg 'Maternal language style', 'West Indian slang', 'Social class difference in speech'

Jis   Continuous assessment
        BT   Assessment

Lik   Portfolio
        BT   Educational publication
        SN   Archive teaching units, eg Jackdaws

Lmh   Multimedia kit
        BT   Collection
        SN   eg Schools Council Concept seven nine

LEC is used as the basis of the classification of the small reference library at the Schools Council, London. Many amendments are made to meet the council's special needs, some of which have been described in an article by Ian McCullough and Patience Edney.[26] The following examples show some of the amendments together with the original LEC:

Schools Council		*LEC2*
Ban	Sociology of education, Sociology of the school	Ban
Band	School as social unit, organic community	—
Bant	School organization, structure	—
Bat	Environment	Bat
Bats	Playgrounds, recreation out of school	—
Jdb	Teacher or school—community, relationship with social environment	Jdb
Jde	Teacher/class relationship, interaction	—
Jdh	Parent-child relation	Jdh
Jdv	Teacher-educand relation, Atmosphere of school, Authority, Discipline, Morale	Jdv
Jdz	Teacher/teacher relationship	—

Very detailed classification is practised, with rotation of facets and a simple specific subject index in visible index form. If information is required on curriculum development, one first checks the visible index and finds

Curriculum development, design, planning Mabb.

In the classified sequence there are cards for all books allotted the class number Mabb, the entries being grouped so that those for which Mab is the first facet are filed first, followed by those for which it is the second facet, those for which it is the third facet and so on (see figure 10).

130

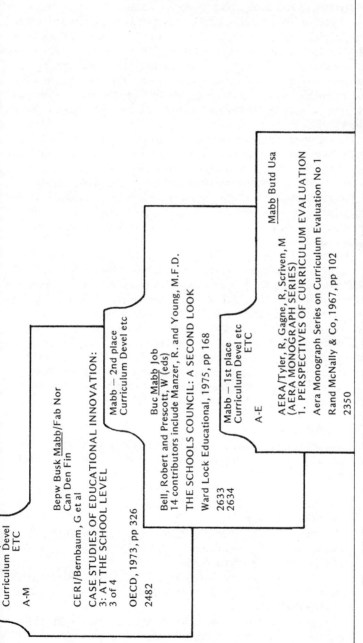

Figure 10: Extracts from the Schools Council's classified catalogue, arranged by the London Education Classification, showing rotation of facets

A book containing information on many topics is given a class mark to represent each topic. For example, *Team teaching in Britain* by John Freeman (Ward Lock, 1968) is classified at Lah (Team teaching) Bep (Planning of education) Raj (Primary schools) Reg (Grammar schools) Rej (Comprehensive schools) Bul (Comparative education) Usa (with USA). Thus the reader wanting information on primary, grammar or comprehensive schools can locate this book via the classified catalogue even though it is classified on the shelf under team teaching. It is up to the book's own index to allow easy location of the relevant sections.

This depth indexing, combined with rotation of entries, could cause problems of bulk in the card catalogue but as yet the collection is not big enough for this to be a serious difficulty. The simplicity of the system and the specificity which it allows make it popular with users.

The card catalogue, which originally included only books, was later expanded to include material housed in the Schools Council Project Information Centre; this material comprises books, teaching kits and audio-visual aids.

The thesaurus section of LEC has been used for the subject index of *Register of educational research in the United Kingdom 1973-1976*, compiled by the National Foundation for Educational Research under a grant from the Department of Education and Science and the Social Science Research Council. The *Register* combines thirty research registers previously published separately. Arrangement is by institution, with an alphabetical index in which the LEC keywords are combined but with no prescribed citation order. Thus a report from Manchester University on non-attendance at school is given the following index entries (1256 is the number of the document and M159 is the register number for Manchester University):

TRUANCY 1256
    School phobia. Attendance. Parent-child relation. City. Rural
    school. Suburb. Sex (biological status). Behaviour   M159
SCHOOL PHOBIA 1256
    Truancy. Attendance. Parent-child relation. City. Rural school.
    Suburb. Sex (biological status). Behaviour   M159
ATTENDANCE 1256
    Truancy. School phobia. Parent-child relation. City. Rural
    school. Suburb. Sex (biological status). Behaviour   M159
PARENT-CHILD RELATION 1256
    Truancy. School phobia. Attendance. City. Rural school.
    Suburb. Sex (biological status). Behaviour   M159
ATTENDANCE 1256
    Truancy. School phobia. Parent-child relation. City. Rural
    school. Suburb. Sex (biological status). Behaviour   M159

CITY 1256
　　Truancy. School phobia. Attendance. Parent-child relation.
　　Rural school. Suburb. Sex (biological status). Behaviour　M159
RURAL SCHOOL 1256
　　Truancy. School phobia. Attendance. Parent-child relation.
　　City. Suburb. Sex (biological status). Behaviour　　　M159
SUBURB 1256
　　Truancy. School phobia. Attendance. Parent-child relation.
　　City. Rural school. Sex (biological status). Behaviour　M159
SEX (BIOLOGICAL STATUS) 1256
　　Truancy. School phobia. Attendance. Parent-child relation. City.
　　Rural school. Suburb. Behaviour　　　　　　　　　　　M159
BEHAVIOUR
　　Truancy. School phobia. Attendance. Parent-child relation.
　　City. Rural school. Suburb. Sex (biological status)　　　M159
LEC 2 was used as the basis for the *EUDISED thesaurus*, and is also
believed to have been adopted by the Irish Department of Education.
There are a number of articles on the use of LEC1.[28]

*Classification Research Group classification of library and information
science*
　　The Classification Research Group's *Classification of library and
information science* (CRG)[29] was originally published in draft form in
1965 as *Classification of library science*. In spite of a number of disadvantages—such as a complicated notation, inadequate treatment of
fringe topics and a very poor index—it was adopted for *Library and
information science abstracts* (LISA) from 1969.
　　Apart from considerable dissatisfaction with the notation, many
users did not like the original citation order which was based on Ranganathan's PMEST formula: type of library, materials (stock), operations, agents, properties, space, time. Following demands from users of
LISA the citation order was changed in the revised edition to: operations, agents, stock, library systems, library users, properties, space,
time. The following examples show the different treatments in the two
editions:

	First ed	*Second ed*
Cataloguing in public libraries	Vs Hm (Public libraries—cata- loguing)	U-HT (Cata- loguing—Public libraries)
Post-co-ordinate indexing of report literature in special libraries	Sd Ly J (Special libraries— Reports— Post-co-ordin- ate indexing)	WVB-LX-JS (Post-co-ordin- ate indexing— Reports—Special libraries)

Teaching Dewey DC in science and technology	M(5/6)Hkg (DEW) Bgd (Sci-tech materials—DC— Teaching)	WQJ RD-N5-EG (DC—Sci-tech materials— Teaching)

It will be seen that in some ways the notation is now even more complex than it was in the first edition and the use of capital letters only means that a facet indicator (—) is now necessary. There is, however, a facility for retroactive notation within each main class, as shown in the following examples:

PM	Library personnel
PME K	Graduates
PME Q	Chiefs
PMK H	Females
PSS	Salary scales
PSS MEK	for graduates
PSS MEQ	for chiefs
PSS MKH	for females

Fringe subjects (called related fields) are now classified at Y but not in any depth. Note 3.2 in the introduction recommends that a general scheme (preferably the revised BC) is needed to do adequate justice to fringe topics.

There is a considerable improvement in the use of scope notes, which are introduced by an asterisk, thus:

X Automatic indexing = Automatic text analysis = Automatic content analysis
   * To be distinguished from mechanized indexing which involves machine assistance of substantially manual/intellectual operations. Automatic indexing here implies the use of the machine to perform entirely the analysis of the information content of documents and the derivation of index devices by statistical, linguistic, etc methods to develop a complete retrieval language of its own.

Coverage of synonymous terms is also good. The above example of automatic indexing illustrates this. Another example is:

WVB Post-co-ordinate indexing = Co-ordinate indexing = Correlative indexing = Manipulative indexing

The index is also very much improved, but the opportunity to use the Thesaurofacet approach has been missed.

Unfortunately one must query the value of the revised CRG scheme. The notation of the revision is not used in LISA—for example, Classification is X_i in LISA but WKC in CRG and Automatic indexing is Zp/x in LISA and X in CGR—and the scheme has now been rejected by both the British Library (Library Association Library) and the College of Librarianship Wales.

The Library Association Library adopted CRG in 1966. Although the notation proved complicated, the scheme presented a more logical approach and provided much greater specificity than had been possible with DC. Being a faceted scheme, it was much more flexible than DC and it was a comparatively simple matter to find places for new subjects. When LISA began to use CRG in 1969, a possible advantage for users was that class numbers in LISA and in the Library Association Library might be the same. This was not, however, always the case and it stopped being so completely in 1971, when LISA adopted the draft revision of CRG. The need to reclassify, coupled with dissatisfaction with the revised CRG scheme, led to the adoption of the eighteenth edition of DC in 1976.

In June 1973 Douglas Ball, librarian of the College of Librarianship Wales (CLW), presented a report to his committee which put forward the following arguments against the adoption of the revised CRG:

1 Those concerned with classifying in CLW library are unanimous in rejecting this as a real improvement on the existing scheme. Whilst the revised overall citation order represents an improvement, the treatment of the previous 'fringe' topics is an accentuation rather than a solution of present problems. The notation in its present form is not acceptable for compatability reasons, but in certain ways has improved on the previous scheme (though the grafting of UDC divisions remains in modified form). However, it remains the scheme which best meets the need for close classification in our special subject field (though for related subjects it is probably the worst); albeit as a classification it is better suited to an abstract journal than a library.

2 The previous scheme has had few proponents and many opponents: I have no reason to believe that the new scheme will convert the unconverted. Its advantage in demonstrating a faceted classification is, in my opinion, more than neutralised by the fact that users have not met it elsewhere prior to coming to CLW and are very unlikely to once they leave.[30]

The final sentence of the first of these points seems to sum up the situation as regards CRG: it is better suited to an abstract journal than a library.

London Classification of Business Studies

LCBS[31] was compiled by K D C Vernon and Valerie Lang at the London Business School, supported financially by a grant of £5,000 from the Office for Scientific and Technical Information (OSTI). The need for a new system to control and organize the literature of business studies was urgently felt at that time, with a rapid development of business schools and business libraries and particularly the establishment in 1965 of graduate business schools at London and Manchester.

Reflecting a tentative definition of business information suggested by the OSTI Business Information Group, the main classes were grouped within three main categories as follows:

MANAGEMENT RESPONSIBILITY WITHIN THE ENTERPRISE

A   Management
AZ   The enterprise
B   Marketing
C   Production
D   Research and development
E   Finance
F   Personnel
G   Office services

ENVIRONMENTAL STUDIES

J   Economics
JZ   Transport
K   Industries
L   Behavioural sciences
M   Communication
N   Education
P   Law
Q   Political science
R   Science and technology
S   Philosophy, logic and scientific method

ANALYTICAL TECHNIQUES

T   Operational research
U   Statistics
V   Mathematics
W   Automation and computers
X   Organization and methods and work study

There are auxiliary schedules for People and occupational roles (schedule one), Industrial products and services (schedule two), Common properties (schedule three), Common activities (schedule four), Geographical divisions (schedule five), Time (schedule six), Form divisions (schedule seven) and Language (schedule eight).

The letters I and O were deliberately omitted in order to avoid confusion with 0 and 1. It will be noted that Z is used as a 'repeater' (rather like 9 in the Colon Classification). The recommended citation order is alphabetical, except that A is always cited last (to avoid overloading the Management class) and P is normally cited first (in order to collect everything on law). Class numbers are combined with an oblique stroke, so that EE/KAA is the class number for financial

136

management in the agricultural industry, where EE is financial management and KAA is the agricultural industry.

LCBS is now known to be used in at least forty British libraries and twenty-two overseas libraries,[32] the users including business schools, government departments, management institutes, training boards, and industrial and commercial concerns. It was incorporated, with modifications, into Thesaurofacet, and it has been translated into French. Degrees of use vary: for example, the Institute of Personnel Management and the London and Manchester business schools use it for shelf arrangement and a classified catalogue; the Oxford Centre for Management Studies also uses it for periodical articles and cuttings files; while other organizations like the Business Archives Council and The City University's Business School use it only for a card index of information or a vertical file.

Many of the users have made their own amendments. For example, Beecham Products have amended class B (Marketing) and expanded class K (Industries) to include their range of products, while two libraries—the Civil Service Department's Central Management Library, and Manchester Business School—have used the vacant class Y for Library and information science, a surprising omission from a scheme which includes so many fringe topics.

Manchester Business School (MBS) has also amended the notation considerably, rejecting the completely hierarchical notation of the original in order to achieve greater brevity and hospitality. The following example illustrates the change:

LCBS		MBS
FE	Conditions of employment	FH
FEB	Hours of work	FHA
FEBB	Full-time	FHB
FEBBB	Shorter working week	FHC

The changes made by users pinpointed certain weaknesses of the scheme, and a seminar for users held at the London Business School in 1973 decided that there should be a thorough revision rather than piecemeal expansion and ad hoc changes. A small working party was set up to carry out this revision, and one of its first acts was to organize a questionnaire survey of the reactions of users (and some non-users). The following were among the comments made:

'More explanatory notes should be included in the schedules to make it easier for even students to use, otherwise the scheme is good'

'At times the classification proves to be too general for our needs, but usually there is room for a breakdown'

'A very useful and timely scheme'

'LCBS will probably be adopted in due course. It seems to have greater flexibility than UDC in this particular area and can give more logical collocation in the area of business and management'

'I did think seriously of using the scheme, which would be extremely applicable for this library. However we did not (in 1971) have the resources to reclassify existing stock. In addition there are advantages in all the polytechnic libraries using the same scheme (ie DC 18). I have used it as an authority list/thesaurus of a kind in generating headings/keywords for our dictionary catalogue: it's been valuable for this purpose.'

'We are using UDC and it is very difficult to change a big library. Otherwise I well know the advantages of LCBS.'

The revision was given a new impetus in 1976 with the award of a grant from the Social Science Research Council, and it is anticipated that the revised edition will be published in 1978. Although it is being produced under the direction of an 'academic' (the writer of this book), working in very close collaboration with the original compilers, it will take account of practical rather than theoretical needs. The notation will be non-hierarchical and there will be alternative treatments and locations where appropriate. There will be many more scope notes, as requested by a number of users. Finally, it will adopt a 'thesauro-facet' approach, so that it will be applicable to pre-co-ordinate and post-co-ordinate systems.

The ANBAR Decimal Classification

The final scheme to be examined in this section is a classification developed for the five abstracting journals on management published by Anbar Publications,[33] which has also been adopted by some libraries. There are four major facets in this scheme:

1 Users (eg industries, research organizations, professional services)
2 Techniques
3 Applications
4 Equipment, Supplies, Services

Each facet is then divided into up to ten subdivisions, thus:

1.2   Transport and distribution
1.20   Road transport
1.21   Air transport
1.22   Shipping, Docks, Harbours
1.23   Communications (excl Post Office)
1.24   Wholesale trade
1.25   Retail trade
1.26   Co-operative movement
1.27   Catering, Hotels, Tourism
1.28   Sundry

2.3   Work study/O & M (Work measurement)
2.30   Simple timing. Averaging

2.32   Sampling
2.33   Time study. Rating
2.35   Predetermined time systems
2.36   Relaxation and other allowances
2.37   Incentives (excl Production incentives—see 3.52)
2.38   Work planning (excl Network—see 3.64)
2.39   Sundry

3.6   Training
3.60   Management development, In-house
3.61   Management development, External
3.62   Supervisors
3.63   Sales force
3.64   Apprentices and students
3.65   Operators/workers
3.66   Training techniques
3.67   Retraining, Impact of automation
3.68   Government agencies, Cost of training
3.69   Sundry

4.2   Audio-visual aids
4.20   Visual aids
4.21   Films and videotape
4.22   Planning board, Wallchart
4.29   Sundry

An article on a multi-faceted topic which has been abstracted in one of the ANBAR journals will be indexed under each facet. Thus, an article on the use of videotape for training supervisors in the air transport industry is indexed under 1.21, 3.62 and 4.21. An alphabetical subject index assists ready location of items in the classified sequence.

The ANBAR Classification is a broad one which is not intended for library use. It works admirably for the retrieval of information from abstracting journals but would have obvious limitations if applied to a large library. One small library which applies it successfully, however, is that of the Institute of Practitioners in Work Study, Organization and Methods (a body which, incidentally, sponsors one of the ANBAR journals, *Work study + O & M abstracts*). The two and a half thousand books contained in this library are classified and shelved by the ANBAR class number, extended where appropriate to accommodate more specific topics than are catered for in the ANBAR classification. Periodical articles which have been abstracted in the ANBAR publications are filed numerically by the ANBAR abstract numbers. A separate card index is also maintained of articles and other information not abstracted in the ANBAR journals but considered to deserve indexing within the institute, and these articles are filed in classified order. No attempt is made to combine the class numbers for multi-faceted topics, but a separate card is made for each facet. For example an article entitled 'What does management by objectives have to do with MTM?' is classified at 2.35 (Methods-Time-Measurement) and 2.03 (Management by objectives) and a letter on multiple regression analysis for clerical work measurement is classified at 2.35 (Clerical work measurement) and 2.69 (Regression analysis). Different coloured cards are used for books (yellow), journal articles abstracted in the ANBAR journals (green), other journal articles (blue) and documents (pink).

Some minor amendments are made to the ANBAR Classification, and where a class number covers several subjects the cards for these subjects are arranged in separate sequences. For example, there are three sequences at 2.52 for Ecology, Ergonomics and Pollution. This is similar to the feature headings which used to be a feature of the *British national bibliography*.

This is a good example of the use within a library of a classification scheme which is used for the major abstracting service in the field, thus assisting in bibliographical control and reference service by ensuring an almost identical arrangement in the abstracting journals and the library's classified catalogue.

Conclusion

Replying to Derek Langridge's criticisms of the article quoted at the beginning of this chapter, Line and Bryant said 'There are, we know, lots of minor classification schemes. How many of these take account of practical as well as theoretical needs? How do they work as shelf classifications from the user's point of view? The existence of a lot of little-known schemes is in any case small help to the general library.'[34]

I have tried to demonstrate in this chapter that a) special schemes are only minor in the sense that they are less widely used than the major schemes like DC, UDC and LC—within their limits such schemes can be very significant; b) the compilers of such schemes generally do attempt to take account of practical needs; c) while some schemes appear to work well for shelf arrangement, others are more suitable for retrieval of information via a classified catalogue, post-co-ordinate index or bibliography; and d) the use of special schemes is not confined to the special library, some general schemes finding them helpful for parts of their stock. There are many special classification schemes—far more than I have been able to cover in this chapter—and most of them appear to have practical value.

References
1 Line, Maurice B and Bryant, Philip 'How golden is your retriever? thoughts on library classification' *Library Association record* 71(5) May 1969, 135-138.
2 Fegan, E S and Cant, M *The Cheltenham classification* 2nd ed. Cambridge, Heffer, 1958.
3 Campbell, Alasdair 'Classification schemes in school libraries' *School librarian* 22(4) December 1974, 310-316.
4 Rash,. J P Letter to the editor *Library resources and technical services* 9(4) fall 1965, 416.
5 National Library of Medicine *National Library of Medicine classification: a scheme for the arrangement of books in the field of medicine and its related sciences* 3rd ed. Bethesda (Maryland), 1969.
6 Scheerer, George and Hines, Lois E 'Classification systems used in medical libraries' *Bulletin of the Medical Library Association* 62(3) July 1974, 273-280.
7 Sophanodorn, Kanchana 'Problems of the National Library of Medicine Classification for serials' *Library resources and technical services* 15(4) fall 1971, 452-457.
8 Jenkins, S R 'British medical libraries today' *Library Association Medical Section bulletin* (107) 1976, 5-6.
9 Library Association, Medical Section *Directory of medical libraries in the British Isles* 4th ed. London, Library Association, 1976.
10 Wessex Medical Library *A brief guide to the classification used in the library* Southampton, University Library, 1972. (Wessex Medical Library, publications series, no 1).
11 Hulme, E Wyndham 'Principles of book classification' *Library Association record* 13, 1911, 354-358, 389-394, 444-449; 14, 1912, 39-46, 174-181, 216-221.
12 Sandison, A 'The special needs of a classification for books and journals' (Paper given at an FID symposium on classification, November 1976, to be published 1977/78).
13 Hulme, E Wyndham: op cit p 216.
14 Coates, E J *The British catalogue of music classification* London, Council of the British National Bibliography, 1960.
15 Long, Maureen W *Musicians and libraries in the United Kingdom* London, Library Association, 1972.
16 McColvin, Lionel Roy and Reeves, Harold *Music libraries* completely rewritten and extended by Jack Dove. London, Deutsch, 1965. vol 1, pp 48-61.
17 Aitchison, Jean, Gomersall, Alan and Ireland, Ralph (comps) *Thesaurofacet: a thesaurus and faceted classification for*

engineering and related topics. Whetstone (Leics), English Electric Company, 1969.

18 Personal communication from Susan Spriggs.

19 *Thesaurus of engineering and scientific terms* New York, Engineers' Joint Council, 1967.

20 Widdowson, J S 'Technical Help for Exporters: the why and how' *The information scientist* 7(3) September 1973, 89-100.

21 Foskett, D J and Foskett, Joy *The London education classification: a thesaurus/classification of British educational terms* 2nd ed. London, University of London Institute of Education Library, 1974. (*Education libraries bulletin,* supplement 6).

22 Personal communication from Geoffrey Dixon.

23 Neill, A G 'The new London Education Classification and the-saurus: a critique' *Education libraries bulletin* 17(3) autumn 1974, 11-20.

24 Stuart-Jones, E A L 'Education classification: some basic problems and the *London Education Classification*' *Education libraries bulletin* (36) autumn 1969, 2-17.

25 Pickles, Stephen 'Using LEC2 to index a pilot study of the computer generation of catalogues to a thesis collection' *Education libraries bulletin* 19(3) autumn 1976, 22-25.

26 McCulloch, Ian and Edney, Patience 'The information services and library of the Schools Council' *Education libraries bulletin* 19(1) spring 1976, 1-12.

27 *EUDISED multilingual thesaurus for information processing in the field of education* prepared by Jean Viet for the council of Europe Documentation Centre for Education in Europe. First English edition 1973. Paris, Mouton, 1974.

28 For example Greaves, Monica A 'The London Education Classi-fication: some practical aspects' *Education libraries bulletin* (25) spring 1966, 13-17; Neill, A G 'The London Education Classification at Didsbury College' *Education libraries bulletin* (38) summer 1970, 1-11.

29 Classification Research Group *A classification of library and information science* by Ruth Daniel and J Mills with the assis-tance of R Selwood and Pirkka Elliott. London, Library Association, 1975. (Library Association, research publication, no 15).

30 Ball, Douglas 'Report to the library committee by the librarian on a classification for CLW library' Aberystwyth, 1973.

31 Verson, K D C and Lang, Valerie *The London classification of business studies* London, London Graduate School of Business Studies, 1970.

32 Bakewell, K G B and Cotton, D A (comps) *The London classifi-
    cation of business studies: an introduction and directory of
    users* 2nd ed. Liverpool, Liverpool Polytechnic Department of
    Library and Information Studies, 1977. (DOLIS occasional
    paper no 7, revised).
33 *Accounting + data processing abstracts, Marketing + distribu-
    tion abstracts, Peronnel + training abstracts, Top management
    abstracts, Work study + O and M abstracts.*
34 Line, Maurice B and Bryant, Philip, Letter to the editor *Library
    Association record* 72(2) February 1970, 72.

Chapter Seven

THE ALPHABETICAL SUBJECT APPROACH:
PRE-CO-ORDINATE

Chain indexing

IN BRITISH LIBRARIES chain indexing remains a popular method of facilitating retrieval via a classified catalogue. Introduced by Ranganathan as an integral part of his Colon Classification and popularized by BNB between 1950 and 1970, there have been many descriptions of this technique[1] and its advantages are now well-known. Suzanne Hicks has described how she adopted chain indexing with a UDC catalogue at the library of Western Australia's government railways after reading Mills's classic articles.[2] She pinpoints four particular advantages of the system: a) intellectual economy because of its link with the classification scheme; b) its systematic approach; c) it indicates the strengths and weaknesses of the classification; d) it alerts the classifier to the need or otherwise for permutation in the classified sequence.

There had been no reader reaction at the time Ms Hicks wrote her article, but she does draw attention to the possible problem of referring to a broader class number (ie a higher link in the chain) when the library only has a document on a more specific aspect, thereby giving the impression that the subject index entry leads nowhere. This should not be a major difficulty with a scheme like UDC, which uses a structural notation, but it could create problems with BC and LC. For example, in the revised BC a document on the teaching of educationally subnormal persons is classified at JVM, subordinated to the teaching of mentally handicapped persons at JVK. The following chain index entries would be generated for this document:

Educationally subnormal persons: Education   JVM
Mentally handicapped persons: Education   JVK

It is not clear that JVM is a subdivision of JVK and the entry for mentally handicapped persons could be misleading if no documents have been classified at JVK. The solution is to make the entry as follows:

Mentally handicapped persons: Education   JVK-JVP

A major advantage of chain indexing is that it ensures the collocation of aspects of a subject which have been scattered in the classification scheme (ie 'distributed relatives') because the last link in the class number is always the first link in the chain of subject index entries. The following examples from the University of Bradford's computer-produced subject index illustrates this:

Water: Atmosphere: Climatology	P551.57
Water: Economic geography	C910.13391
Water: Hydraulic engineering	X626/627
Water: Inorganic chemistry	N546.212
Water: Natural resources: Economics	E333.91
Water: Physical geography	P551.46
Water: Pollution: Public health engineering	X628.19
Water: Supply: Engineering	X628.1
Water: Supply: Economics	E338.277
Water: Transport	E386

(As explained on page 17, the initial letter indicates the main section of the library where the subject will be found and this is followed by the DC or UDC class number.) The computer at Bradford produces not only an alphabetical printout but also a classified printout which acts as an authority file for classifiers and is also available for public consultation.

The library of South Trafford College of Further Education, Altrincham, has a classified catalogue with an alphabetical subject index compiled by chain procedure.[3] It is, however, a subject index with a difference since it not only refers to the classified catalogue for books on a particular subject but also lists periodicals and audio-visual materials which contain information on that subject. The periodicals are arranged by accession number within forms of material. The front of the card contains a grid which enables the user to see at a glance what materials the library has on each subject, blank spaces being left for any new media additions such as overhead projector transparencies. The reverse of the card indicates where these materials are located. A typical card appears at figure eleven.

It may be argued that, since each form of NBM is arranged numerically, a post-co-ordinate indexing system would have been more useful. This was considered but rejected, partly because of its complexity but also, more importantly, because it would have meant asking library users to consult an additional index for non-book materials. There is great virtue in having to consult only one index although it is recognized that, unlike a post-co-ordinate system, this index will not allow immediate retrieval of items on multi-faceted topics such as the effect of pollution on plant life. This is not considered a great disadvantage, as it is no real hardship to consult all the items on plant life or pollution and could indeed be a positive advantage.

Allen F Armsby, South Trafford's tutor-librarian, who devised the grid system, is sometimes asked what happens when there is no more

Environment

DETAILS ON BACK OF CARD

BOOKS	●	RECORDS	
CASSETTES (AUDIO)	●	SLIDES	
CHARTS	●	SUPPLEMENTS	
CUTTINGS		TAPES	
FILMS		VIDEOTAPES	
FILMS (LOOPS)			
FILMSTRIPS	●		
PERIODICALS	●		
PROJECT FILES	●		

Front of card. Dots are inserted with a red felt-tipped pen and indicate that there are books, cassettes, charts, filmstrips, periodicals, and project files on the environment.

BOOKS: 574.5

CASSETTES: C97, C99

CHARTS: Ch91, Ch92, Ch96, Ch97

FILMSTRIPS: 12, 62, 97, 221, 302, 307

PERIODICALS: Bulletin of environmental
                education
            Environment & change

PROJECT FILES: P/F574.5, P/F711.4

Reverse of card. This indicates that books are classified at 574.5 on the shelves and in the classified catalogue, and gives the titles of relevant periodicals and numbers of audio-visual material.

Figure 11: Subject index card, South Trafford College of Further Education

room on a card. He has to reply that he does not know as it has not yet happened, but it should be possible to provide a continuation card.

The grid system combines simplicity with practical usefulness and is easily understood by library users, who impressed me on my visit with their lively appreciation of what the library could do for them. It has since been adopted with local variations by a number of other libraries and resource centres including the Abraham Moss Centre in Manchester, Manchester Public Libraries' Educational Precinct Library, and schools in Rochdale and Derbyshire.

In addition to the specific subject index there is also a 'thematic index' of NBM arranged under broad headings corresponding to the teaching interests of the college and thus allowing lecturers to see at a glance the range of audio-visual materials available to them without having to decide specific topics. The headings used are: Art and design; Biology; Economics; Education; Environment; Food and catering; Geography: Great Britain; Geography: world; History: Great Britain; History: world; Mathematics and computing; Medical; Music; Music: composers; Poetry, prose and plays; Psychology; Religion; Society and government; Space; Sport; Technology; Transport.

A library which does not use chain indexing (except in the Edinburgh room) is Edinburgh City Libraries. Although the central reference library has a dictionary catalogue, the branch libraries and other service points in the central library, apart from the reference department in the Scottish Library, all have classified catalogues supported by a printed subject index (*Subject and name index of books contained in the libraries*. 3rd ed 1949, and cumulated supplement, 1949-1965, 1966 and amendment sheets.) The following are examples of entries from this index:

Police, African S	HV8271
Argentina, reports	HV7689
Australian	HV8280
Canadian North West Mounted	F1060
Colonial, service list	wJV1073P
Edinburgh	YHV8198
English history	HV8195
English, life in	HV8195
English, methods	HV8195
English, women	HV7625
Women	HV8023

It will be seen that, as in the index to the LC schedules, there is much repetition in this index. Several of the entries refer to HV and the use of chain indexing would have produced considerable economies throughout.

Entries are also provided under more specific headings, thus:

Australia
  police   HV8280
Canadian North West Mounted Police   F1060
Women
  police   HV8023
  police, Eng   HV7625

The fine art library maintains its own subject index in sheaf form for books, slides, illustrations and information files, as does the Edinburgh Library. The following are examples of entries from the sheaf subject index in the fine art library:

SUDLEY [House]: The Emma Holt bequest to
  Liverpool Corporation   N1410S
WASHINGTON—National Gallery of Art   N857
  Sculpture   NB25 W31
  Exhibitions   N5020 W31

(Note also the use of the Anglo-American code of 1908 here. According to AACR 1967, British text, the National Gallery of Art would be entered directly under its name and not under Washington. Although AACR is, of course, a code for author-title cataloguing, the same rules would apply to names of persons, places and corporate bodies in the subject index.)

Conventional alphabetical subject headings

In the United States the dictionary catalogue remains predominant, using a list of subject headings such as that produced by the Library of Congress (LCSH)[4] as a guide (or sometimes as a bible) for the establishment of headings.

Dorothy Kanwischer's questionnaire survey in 1974 has produced some interesting information about the attitudes of 108 US university libraries to LCSH.[5] Although 78.2 per cent of the 108 respondents considered LCSH adequate for users, thirty-five per cent changed their headings in some way, many of these changes consisting of added cross-references. Eleven libraries (10.8 per cent) complained about time-lag in LC's acceptance of new terms and phrases. Other complaints concerned poor coverage of local history (eight respondents), education (seven), theology (four), sociology (three) and academic theses (three). As an illustration of the fact that nothing will please everybody all the time, one library said the headings were too broad while another complained that they were too specific. There were complaints about clumsy, inverted and confused headings, and the traditional differences in punctuation—commas for inverted headings, dashes for subdivisions and parentheses for scope notes—were criticized as being misleading to users.

Almost half the respondents had a divided catalogue (separate sequences for authors and subjects), and ninety per cent considered this an improvement. One library had a three-way division (author, title, subject) and another had a four-way division (author, title, subject, series).

As an illustration of the peculiarities of LCSH, Ms Kanwischer quotes some 'odd' headings like COMMANDMENTS, TEN; FROGS — ADDRESSES, ESSAYS, LECTURES; ONE-LEG RESTING POSITION; and SEE, HOLY see HOLY SEE. In contrast she quotes several important headings which have had to be added by her library, University of the Pacific, because they are not in LCSH, such as POLICE CORRUPTION; SEX DISCRIMINATION; and THIRD WORLD.

Edinburgh City Libraries uses LCSH for the dictionary catalogues in its Scottish department and central reference library. An example of a subject entry appears as figure twelve.

UNITED STATES: Foreign Relations: China

    KUBECK, Anthony. How the Far East was lost: American policy and the creation of Communist China, 1941-1949. 1971. 9.2 in.

E183.8C5

Bibliog.

Figure 12: Entry from dictionary catalogue, Edinburgh City Libraries

One of the advantages of using Library of Congress subject headings is the fact that they are included on UK and LC MARC tapes, and this is why Boston University Library ceased to be one of the few American libraries to have a classified catalogue in July 1972.[6] It was decided from that date to accept LC call numbers and subject headings as on MARC tapes received via the Ohio College Library Center (OCLC) and the New England Library Network (NELINET). The classified catalogue had been operational since September 1948, and Margaret Hazen reported that it was not without regret that it was discontinued as it had served the university well for many years and the problems involved in its maintenance had been accompanied by very real benefits. These benefits included flexibility in terminology, the possibility of displaying additional relationships and subject aspects, the ease with which terminology could be updated since only the index cards needed to be changed, and economy of cards since two LC subject headings were often covered by one class number. Problems included the fact that maintenance of the catalogue was time-consuming, the lengthy period of training needed for new staff, and the lack of a general index to the LC schedules which sometimes made it difficult to provide subject headings for class numbers.

The new catalogue seems to have been accepted by readers. 'Some people swear by it, some people swear at it', writes Ms Hazen, 'but mostly readers just use it.' The reference staff apparently find it a useful tool.

Peter Enyingi has surveyed the subject heading practices of two hundred US law libraries, 85.5 per cent of which use LCSH.[7] Only 16.5 per cent, however, accept the subject headings as they stand, a frequent modification being a breakdown of the general heading LAW, described by one librarian as a 'drawer-clogger that no law student would approach, a disservice to law librarians and a frustration.' Other criticisms of published lists concerned terminology, described variously as 'inconsistent, vague, outdated, not specific enough, too specific, and prejudiced'; maintenance and time-lag between editions; inadequate scope notes; unresponsiveness to social change; poor provision for foreign law; and insufficient cross-references. Sixty-six of the two hundred libraries were using more than one list of subject headings in combination.

A popular subject headings list among medical libraries is the National Library of Medicine's (NLM's) *MeSH (Medical subject headings)*,[8] used for the headings of *Index medicus*. McNutt and Poland have described the conversion of the catalogue of Albany Medical College, Albany, New York, from LCSH to MeSH in 1972.[9] At the same time a three-way division of the catalogue took place (proper names, titles, subjects) and various other changes were introduced including the use of a guide card system to eliminate the typing of subject headings on individual catalogue cards and the use of reverse chronological order as the subordinate filing arrangement under subjects. Reasons for making the change included the fact that MeSH is revised annually and the possibility it provided of making more effective use of NLM centralized cataloguing services. The point is also made that the timing of the change was satisfactory, the stock still being sufficiently small (84,000 cards) to allow complete conversion. Much use was made during the conversion of Thelma Charen's *MEDLARS indexing manual*.[10]

Another library which uses MeSH because of NLM's cataloguing services, especially CATLINE (cataloguing on-line) is that of the School of Public Health and Tropical Medicine, Sydney.[11]

The College of Physicians of Philadelphia library divided its ninety-year-old dictionary catalogue by date because of overcrowding, obsolete subject headings, and the lack of a complete authority list as a result of which like materials were being scattered throughout the catalogue under several headings.[12]   The result was two catalogues—a current catalogue for post-1950 publications and an historical biographical catalogue.   The current catalogue was further divided into name and subject catalogues, and the subject section was revised according to MeSH.

For its alphabetical subject catalogue the Wessex Medical Library uses MeSH completely unmodified apart from the substitution of British spellings for American spellings (such as ANAESTHETICS instead of ANESTHETICS and PAEDIATRICS instead of PEDIATRICS). A typical entry appears at figure thirteen, and it will be seen that there is no author heading as the Wessex Medical Library uses the 'alternative headings' method of cataloguing instead of traditional main and added entries.

Some libraries in the Wessex region have used a separate list for British organisations.   Rigid use of MeSH, as at the Wessex Medical Library, means that work on the National Health service is catalogued under STATE MEDICINE. Great Britain.

MeSH is also widely used in post-co-ordinate indexing systems and is the index language for the MEDLINE computerized retrieval system.

MENTAL HEALTH. Legislation

The Mental Health Act, 1959, by S. R. Speller.
2nd ed.

London, Institute of Hospital Administrators, 1969.

First edition published as a series in 'The Hospital'.

69-521687

WM32.FA1   WML-GH

Key: 69-521687 = accession number
        WM32.FA1 = class mark (National Library of
                     Medicine classification)
        WML-GH   = location (Wessex Medical Library—
                     General Hospital)

Figure 13: Extract from the alphabetical subject catalogue,
Wessex Medical Library, using 'Medical subject headings'

British technology index-type indexes

In 1960 E J Coates published the most significant book to date on subject cataloguing.[13] Two years later he put some of his ideas into practice when he became the first editor of *British technology index* (BTI).

BTI headings are alphabetical but based on classificatory principles. The 'thing' or 'end-product' (the personality facet in Ranganathan terms) is always the key term in the entry, followed by terms denoting part, property, material or action. Cross-references are made from all other terms which are considered to be sought headings.

The following is the BTI (1970) subject heading for an article on the shrink-resistant finishing of wool materials with polyurethane:

KNITWEAR: Fabrics; Wool, ,Shrink resistant: Finishing: Polyurethane

Cross-references are made in a right-to-left direction, thus:

FABRICS: Knitwear. See KNITWEAR: Fabrics

WOOL; Fabrics: Knitwear. See KNITWEAR: Fabrics; Wool

SHRINK RESISTANT WOOL FABRICS: Knitwear. See KNIT-
WEAR: Fabrics; Wool, ,Shrink resistant

FINISHING: Shrink resistant wool fabrics: Knitwear. See KNIT-
WEAR: Fabrics: Wool, ,Shrink resistant: Finishing

POLYURETHANE: Finishing: Shrink resistant wool fabrics: Knitwear. See KNITWEAR: Fabrics; Wool, ,Shrink resistant: Finishing:
Polyurethane

The distinctive punctuation is deliberate, the colon being used for syntactic relations (ie relations subsisting between the property, action, material or part on the one hand and the thing or entity on the other hand) and the comma for all generic relations (ie those which define or delimit a thing or entity) except in the case of a material, when a semi-colon is used. The double comma indicates that 'shrink resistant' applies to 'wool fabrics' and not simply to 'wool'; had the latter been the case, a single comma would have been used.

BTI headings have been criticized by some for their alleged complexity. However Angela Gould reported in 1974, following a survey of subscribers to *Science abstracts*, that users tend to go to BTI rather than *Engineering index* partly because of its very specific subject headings.[14]

One library which compiled a subject catalogue based on BTI principles is that of the Natural Rubber Producers' Association (now the Malaysian Rubber Producers' Research Association),[15] but this catalogue is now in need of editing to help make it function effectively.[16]

At Metal Box Limited reports, pamphlets, patents and similar materials are arranged numerically, subject retrieval being effected by a computer sorted subject list which is at present produced monthly with annual cumulations. It is anticipated that these cumulations may eventually be produced at three-monthly intervals.

The subject headings are very precise and exemplify the faceted principles of the Colon Classification, which is used for the library's bookstock (see pages 96-9). There are 122 major terms and these are broken down into subheadings which are introduced by distinctive punctuation such as : separating facets and — qualifying by such characteristics as property or type, thus:

DIMENSIONS: OPTICAL CHARACTER RECOGNITION
ENGINEERS: TRAINING
FOIL LAMINATES — GLASS/PLASTICS
FOOD — STORED: PESTS — INSECTS: IDENTIFICATION

Each computer-sorted index consists of the following sections:

0   ORIGINAL REFERENCE INDEX
1   AUTHOR INDEX
2   PATENT NUMBER INDEX
3   FIRM AND TRADE NAME INDEX
4   SUBJECT INDEX

Taking two examples, we find the following entries:

0:/— REPR 1438: : > > AMERICAN PAINT J. 50-53 (17 SEP 73)

1:    CARDEN C. H. : : /— REPR 1438
  :   SMITH O. W. : :/— REPR. 1438
  :   TRECKER D. J. : :/— REPR. 1438

2:    B1322381: BRITISH ALUMINIUM

3:    BRITISH ALUMINIUM: :/— PAT/B1322381

4 (SUBJECT INDEX):
CANS
    — ALUMINIUM: COATINGS — NYLON II: PRIMERS — EP/
      PHENOLIC : :/— PAT/B1322381
          : PRIMERS — EP/PHENOLIC: COATINGS — NYLON
             II : :/— PAT/B1322381
COATINGS
    : CURING — RADIATION/HEAT: :/— REPR 1438
    — NYLON II: CANS — ALUMINIUM: PRIMERS — EP/
      PHENOLIC : :/— PAT/B1322381
    — PRIMERS — EP/PHENOLIC: CANS — ALUMINIUM: COAT-
      INGS — NYLON II: :/— PAT/B1322381
CURING
    — RADIATION/HEAT: COATINGS: :/— REPR 1438
CURING HEAT
    / RADIATION: COATINGS: :/— REPR 1438

This system has an obvious affinity with the BTI system. Coates, then editor of BTI, did in fact advise on its implementation.

PRECIS

A system which clearly owes something to BTI principles but which has developed along its own lines is PRECIS (PREserved Context Index System), introduced by BNB in 1971 and since adopted by a number of other bibliographies and indexes including *Australian national bibliography*, *British education index*, the Canadian Film Board's *Catalogue supplement*, the British Universities Film Council's *Audio-visual materials in higher education*, and *HELPIS (Higher Education Learning Programmes Information System)* catalogue. There have been several descriptions of the system.[17]

The idea of PRECIS is that a user may enter an alphabetical index at any one of the significant terms which together make up a compound subject statement and there find the full context in which his chosen term has been considered by the author—ie a full statement (a kind of precis) is offered to the user under every term in the subject which the indexer regards as significant enough to be used as an entry word. The system is based on the concept of an open-ended vocabulary, which allows new terms to be admitted into the index at any time once they have been encountered in the literature.

When indexing, a compound subject is broken down into a string of terms summarizing the subject, and a role operator (see figure fourteen) is prefixed to each term. The position of each term in the string is normally determined by the ordinal value of its preceding operator. The indexer is recommended to look first for a term denoting action (role operator two), then to look for the object of the action or key system (role operator one), which may or may not be accompanied by dependent elements. The order of terms achieved by the operators is based on a system of context dependency, each term setting the next term into its obvious context.

Computer instruction codes are added to the string and the computer shunts each term through three basic positions in the index:

Taking a simple example from the *British national bibliography*, a book on sociological perspectives of bilingualism in Canada receives the following subject index entries:

CANADA
    Bilingualism. Sociological perspectives   301.21

Main line operators			
Environment of observed system	0	Location	
Observed system (Core operators)	1	Key system: *object of transitive action; agent of intransitive action*	
	2	Action/Effect	
	3	Agent of transitive action; Aspects; Factors	

A ─────────────────────

Data relating to observer	4	Viewpoint-as-form	
Selected instance	5	Sample population/Study region	
Presentation of data	6	Target/Form	

Interposed operators

Dependent elements	p	Part/Property
	q	Member of quasi-generic group
	r	Aggregate
Concept interlinks	s	Role definer
	t	Author attributed association
Coordinate concepts	g	Coordinate concept

B ─────────────────────

Differencing operators
(prefixed by $)

h	Non-lead direct difference
i	Lead direct difference
j	Salient difference
k	Non-lead indirect difference
m	Lead indirect difference
n	Non-lead parenthetical difference
o	Lead parenthetical difference
d	Date as a difference

Connectives

Components of linking phrases;	v	Downward reading component
(prefixed by $)	w	Upward reading component

C ─────────────────────

Theme interlinks

x	First element in coordinate theme
y	Subsequent element in coordinate theme
z	Element of common theme

Figure 14: PRECIS role operators

BILINGUALISM. Canada
    Sociological perspectives   301.21
    SOCIOLOGICAL PERSPECTIVES. Bilingualism. Canada   301.21
    Just as BNB popularized chain indexing in the 1950s and 1960s,
so its use of PRECIS may well lead to this system being widely used in
libraries, particularly if they have access to computers. Significant
factors are the inclusion of PRECIS strings on UK MARC tapes and
presumably they will also form part of the BLAISE and MERLIN on-
line systems. A survey of indexers' reactions to the system, currently
being undertaken by Liverpool Polytechnic's Department of Library
and Information Studies with financial support from the British
Library's Research and Development Department, indicates that the
system is gradually gaining ground though many indexers are also
critical (and/or perhaps afraid) of it. The following is a selection of
comments made about PRECIS by early respondents to the survey:
'The intellectual process of PRECIS appeals to indexers.'
'It is more rigid than other systems, with less scope for variation by
individual indexers.'
'The specificity of PRECIS is an advantage. Chain indexing is quicker
but less specific.'
'A problem with a PRECIS index to a classified catalogue is that
PRECIS strings cover individual documents but class numbers don't:
it may be necessary to make a long search through class numbers for
specific documents.'
'PRECIS indexing is time-consuming.'
'The bulk of a PRECIS index could become a problem.'
'Because we use PRECIS manually we have to use a simplified form
which means that we cannot 'shunt' all the terms as recommended in
the *Manual*. Therefore it is not fully effective as an indexing system
but still, I would hope, more useful and flexible than chain indexing.'
'We decided to adopt PRECIS when we computerized and consider it
a very effective indexing system, particularly from the index *user's*
point of view. Any reservations we have are over the apparent complexity in *compiling* the index entries and in using the PRECIS *Manual*.'
'PRECIS was considered briefly for the subject index to a classified
catalogue but was rejected as unsuitable for a manual system.'
'The PRECIS index used in BNB is very helpful in searching and a great
improvement on the previous method.'
'As I see it, the great advantage of PRECIS is the ability to manipulate
a string of information terms to produce multiple lead terms for print
out or interrogation.'
'PRECIS entries seem unnecessarily complex, producing a bulky layout
which would require much concentration on the part of the user.'
'It is more expensive to maintain a dictionary catalogue on PRECIS
principles.'

'A PRECIS index would be confusing for public library users.'
'PRECIS entries are often cumbersome, too detailed and unclear.'
The Inner London Education Authority's Central Library Resources Service introduced PRECIS on an operational basis in December 1976, having previously used it in an experimental form. The following is an entry from a cataloguer's worksheet for a filmstrip and pamphlet entitled *Skeleton and muscle*:

$z	1	103	0	$a	animals
$z	2	103	0	$a	movement
$z	s	003	0	$a	role $v of $w in
$z	3	103	0	$a	musculoskeletal system

Reference to figure fourteen shows that ANIMALS is the key system (1), MOVEMENT is the action (2) and MUSCULOSKELETAL SYSTEM is the agent of the action (3). The lower case s is a role definer, $v is an instruction to the computer to add the word 'of' after 'role' when reading downwards and $w tells it to add 'in' when reading upwards. The resulting subject index entries are:

ANIMALS
    Movement. Role of musculoskeletal system   591.1852
MOVEMENT. Animals
    Role of musculoskeletal system   591.1852
MUSCULOSKELETAL SYSTEM. Role in movement.
    Animals   591.1852

A variety of subject indexing systems was used by the constituent libraries of the City of London Polytechnic before the polytechnic's formation in 1970, but these were often of the 'hit or miss' variety. Library of Congress subject headings were used for a time after the adoption of MARC cataloguing services until the introduction of the revised version of PRECIS (PRECIS 2) by the British Library in 1974. PRECIS 2 is now used for all items catalogued by the UK MARC service since 1974 and for all items catalogued locally since March 1976; it has also been applied to some pre-1974 MARC items. The full subject statements provided by PRECIS strings are much preferred by users to Library of Congress subject headings but a problem for indexers is the lack of access to the British Library's authority file. An example from the subject index appears as figure fifteen.

Although PRECIS was designed for computer manipulation it is not, as sometimes imagined, solely of use to libraries with access to a computer. One of the earliest British libraries to use the system—in a simplified manual form—was Sheffield City College of Education (now part of Sheffield City Polytechnic). A book entitled *The moral and physical condition of the working classes employed in the cotton manufacture in Manchester* receives the following subject index entries:

Opinions
   See also
      Attitudes
      Political beliefs
Optical equipment
   See also
      Cameras
Optical equipment
   Optical precision engineering equipment. Construction &
     calibration   681'.4
Optical spectroscopy
   Optical emission spectroscopy   535'.84
Optics
   See also
      Light
Optics   535
Optimal control theory
   Applications in management   658.4'033
Optimal personality   155.2
Optimisation   515
Optimisation. Transport networks
   — Study examples: Road networks — Study regions:
     Netherlands   388'.1'0184
Oral
   See also
      Mouth
Oral communication
   See also
      Public
Oratory See Public speaking
Orbitals. Molecules
   — Festschriften   541'.28
Orbitals. Molecules. Organic compounds
   Symmetry. Conservation — Programmed texts   547'.1'28
Organic acids
   See also
      Nucleic acids
Organic chemistry
   — For biology   547'.002'4574
Organic compounds
   See also
      Carbodydrates
      Cytochromes
      Documents on organic compounds
      Ethylene
      Haemoglobins
      Organometallic compounds
      Proteins
Organic compounds   547
   Absorption spectroscopy   547'.308'5
   Infrared spectroscopy. Spectra — Illustrations   547'.308'5

Figure 15: Extract from the City of London Polytechnic library
subject index, showing the use of PRECIS

MANCHESTER
Cotton manufacturing industries. Personnel. Social
    conditions   301.4442
COTTON MANUFACTURING INDUSTRIES. Manchester
Personnel. Social conditions   301.4442
MANUFACTURING INDUSTRIES. Manchester
Cotton manufacturing industries. Personnel. Social
    conditions   301.4442
PERSONNEL. Cotton manufacturing industries. Manchester
Social conditions   301.4442
SOCIAL CONDITIONS. Personnel. Cotton Manufacturing
industries. Manchester   301.4442

When I visited the library I found that the subject index cards were well thumbed—a clear indication of frequent use. Users are helped by a clear and simple guide to the subject index (see figure sixteen).

Articulated subject indexing

Articulated subject indexes (ASI) consist of subject headings modified by phrases which augment the descriptive subject headings, alphabetized within each subject heading. They are frequently found in 'back of the book' indexes and in indexes to periodicals. Michael Lynch of the University of Sheffield Postgraduate School of Librarianship and Information Science has done a great deal of work on the computer manipulation of such indexes, which began in 1965 with an examination of the subject indexes to *Chemical abstracts* with a view to determining their potential use in computer searches.[18-19] The computer program developed by Lynch has been applied to *SMRE bibliography*[20] and *World textile abstracts*, entries from the 1973 volume of which appear below:

	Abstract no
Fibres	
production of, from films	1888
freezing of solvent solutions for	2848P
from thermoplastic resins,	
Forshaga process for	8746
spinning of	2648
Filaments	
production of, from films	1888
Films	
production of filaments and fibres from	1888
Resins	
thermoplastic, Forshaga process for production	
of fibres from	8746
Spinning	
of fibres	2648

TO OBTAIN BOOKS ON A PARTICULAR SUBJECT

Look in the subject index under the most specific term relating to the main part of the subject.
Check the nearby index entries in case they prove to be helpful.

Index entries give the classification number under which books on the subject (and often related subjects) are listed in the classified file of the catalogue.
For precise information, check this file before going to the shelves.

ARTISTS
  — Biographies   709.22

VISUAL ARTS
  — History   709

But complex subjects are usually listed under all their main aspects.

VISUAL ARTS
  Aesthetics   701.17

AESTHETICS. Visual arts   701.17

When the subject is an important, but subsidiary, theme of a book, an added class reference is made under the classification number for this subject in the classified file of the catalogue, directing the user to the main classified entry.

330.977 see
917.7
AKIN, Wallace Elmus
  The north central United States.

330.977 denotes Economic conditions in the north central United States.
917.7 denotes the general geography of the north central United States.

Figure 16: Guide to the subject index (PRECIS style),
Sheffield City College of Education (now part of Sheffield City Polytechnic)

SLIC indexing

Selective Listing in Combination (SLIC) was introduced by J R Sharp in an effort to retain the advantages of permutation when indexing compound terms but also reducing the number of entries by combining in one direction only and excluding combinations of terms which are included in the larger group.[21] Thus, if an index entry is made for five terms ABCDE there is no need to make entries for ABCD, ABC, AB or A since these are all included in ABCDE. Entries are, however, needed for the following combinations which would otherwise not be traced: ACDE, ADE, AE, BCDE, BDE, BE, CDE, CE, DE, E.

SLIC indexes were produced for internally generated reports at ICI Fibres (Pontypool) between 1967 and 1971. Each index consisted of the following three sections:

1 The thesaurus
2 The index, referring to accession number
3 The accessions register, providing full details of each report.

Since all the reports in the indexes are confidential, it is not possible to provide actual examples but the following entries illustrate the layout:

Computers: Control systems: Machine tools
   866
Computers: Machine tools
   866
Control systems: Machine tools
   866
Machine tools
   866

author	*title*	*date*	*source*	*report/ page no*
Richards, M.	Computer-controlled machine tools in the USA	1970	Machinery, 117	866

Frank X Gagne uses a modified SLIC index in the International Nickel Company of Canada Limited (INCO), and I am grateful to him for permission to quote from a letter and to reproduce some of his entries. He has made two important modifications:

1 In order to avoid an excessive number of combinations and some meaningless entries, not all keywords are used in the index and professional librarians indicate which are to be 'SLICed' (field 240 of figure seventeen). These keywords are chosen from the controlled (field 220) and uncontrolled (field 230) keywords.

2 SLIC keywords are entered on the data entry sheet (figure seventeen) in order of importance. This is significant, as the program is capable of producing entries on any desired number of SLIC keywords. For example the first three keywords from field 240 may be SLICed; if it is

JRGRL I.R. DATA ENTRY SHEET

FILE DESCRIPTOR

ACCESSION NUMBER

PRIMARY   SECONDARY

LOCATION (140)

FORMAT (180)

DATE (130)
y y m m d d

LANG/REST (510)

SUBJECT AREAS (200)

TITLE (110)   SHORTEN IF NECESSARY

CORPORATE AUTHOR (210)

AUTHORS (120)   SURNAME AND TWO INITIALS

1.
2.
3.

PAGINATION (300)

BIBLIOGRAPHIC DESCRIPTION (100)   SOURCE DOCUMENT

CONTROLLED KEYWORDS (220)

1
2
3
4
5
6
7
8
9
10

UNCONTROLLED KEYWORDS (230)

1
2
3
4
5
6
7
8
9
10

CHECK HERE ☐ MORE ON BACK

4
5
6

CHECK HERE ☐ ADDITIONAL SETS ON BACK

SLIC KEYWORDS (240)   IN ORDER OF IMPORTANCE

1
2
3

ABSTRACT (400)

1
2
3
4

CHECK HERE ☐ MORE ON BACK

COMPLETED BY

92-005

Figure 17: Data entry sheet, International Nickel Company of Canada Limited

subsequently found that this generates insufficient specificity, four keywords may be SLICed instead. Alternatively the reverse process is possible.

The basic components of a bibliographic unit are entered on the data entry sheet by clerical assistants. The assigning of basic keywords and the selection of SLIC keywords from these are done by professional librarians.

The SLIC index (figure eighteen) refers to the bibliographic listing in numerical order (figure nineteen). There is also a basic keyword index (figure twenty) and an author index.

KWIC and KWOC indexing

KWIC (keyword-in-context) indexing was originally introduced by Andrea Crestadoro as long ago as 1864, under the name 'Keyword in titles', for a catalogue of Manchester Public Libraries. Nearly a century later it was developed by H P Luhn for computer manipulation[22] and applied to the American Chemical Society's current awareness publication *Chemical titles*. In KWIC indexing, titles are sorted by computer so that each significant word appears in the centre of a column or page in its correct alphabetical sequence surrounded by the words preceding and following it in the title. In KWOC (keyword-out-of-context) indexing, the keyword appears in the margin or in the form of a catalogue heading.

One of the problems of KWIC and KWOC indexes is the non-informative or vague title, which may not generate meaningful keywords and may indeed be positively unhelpful. The Mitre Corporation, McLean, Virginia, has overcome this problem by having the professional indexer add desirable terms for its KWOC index when scanning the library clerk's citation information for accuracy and indicating these additions with an asterisk.[23] A technique has also been developed for providing some pre-co-ordination by linking terms with hyphens: for example, 'The uniform data element description' is indexed under DATA-ELEMENT* as well as DATA, ELEMENT, UNIFORM and DESCRIPTION. This type of indexing is also used to hold together the various elements of a corporate name, eg *SOCIETY-OF-AUTOMO-TIVE-ENGINEERS. A weekly cumulative index, sort and print runs for up to eight hundred documents requires less than five minutes of computer time and master file merge and print runs outputting the complete index had not (up to 1970 when the collection of technical reports in the index totalled 10,000) ever exceeded twelve minutes of computer time.

KWIC and KWOC indexes have been a feature of special libraries, especially industrial libraries, for some years, and Lucille Campey has described thirty-four such indexes developed in the USA, Britain and

163

PAGE 80   VERTICAL FILE: 5468-6795: SLIC

CARBON, REDUCING AGENTS, SUBMERGED ARC FURNACES
    LVF 6,265

CARBON, REMOVAL
    LVF 5,484

CARBON, REMOVAL, STAINLESS STEELS
    LVF 5,483

CARBON, SPECTROSCOPY
    LVF 6,473

CARBON, STAINLESS STEELS
    LVF 5,483

CARBON, SUBMERGED ARC FURNACES
    LVF 6,265

CARBONATES, X-RAYS
    LVF 6,411

CARBON DETERMINATION, PIG IRON, STEEL, SULFUR DETERMINATION
    LVF 6,727

CARBON DETERMINATION, PIG IRON, SULFUR DETERMINATION
    LVF 6,727

CARBON DETERMINATION, STEEL, SULFUR DETERMINATION
    LVF 6,727

CARBON DETERMINATION, SULFUR DETERMINATION
    LVF 6,727

Figure 18: Extract from modified SLIC index, International Nickel Company of Canada Limited

PAGE   14   VERTICAL FILE: 5468-6795: BIBLIOGRAPHIC LISTING

LVF 5.648 TRANSPIRATION METHOD FOR EQUILIBRIUM PRESSURE
           DETERMINATION. TANIGUCHI,M.;KAGAKU TO KOGYO
           (TOKYO).1965.18(S).P.645 (11P).(JAP).(ANAL.
           &.INSTR.)
KEYWORDS: TRANSPIRATION.EQUILIBRIUM PRESSURE.REVIEW

LVF 5.649 ELECTROLYTIC DEPOSITION OF COPPER ON TITANIUM
           AND STEEL BASES.   OPPERMANN,B.;HEIN,K.;LANGE
           ,H.;.NEUE HUETTE.1972.JUN..17(6).P.334 (7P)
           .(GERM)
KEYWORDS: ELECTRODEPOSITION.COPPER.TITANIUM//STEEL.
CATHODE BLANKS

LVF 5.650 CATALYTIC METHODS FOR TRACE METAL ANALYSIS.
           BATLEY,G.E.;.PROC.R.AUST.CHEM.INST..1972.SEP.,
           39(9). P.261 (7P).(CHEM ENG.)
KEYWORDS: CHEMICAL ANALYSIS.CATALYTIC EFFECT//
TRACE METALS.LIGAND EXCHANGE.POLAROGRAPHY.ENZYMES

LVF 5.651 LEACHING OF MINERAL SULFIDES BY SELECTIVE OXI
           DATION AT NORMAL PRESSURE.JORLING,TROY.;I
           NST.TECHNOL.DIV.N.CN-FERROUS METAL..1972.NOV.
           (19P).(HYDROMET.)
LEACHING UNDER MODERATE CONDITIONS ALLOWS RECOVERY OR R
EAGENTS AND IS SUITABLE FOR A VARIETY OF AW MATERIALS.
KEYWORDS: LEACHING.SULFIDES.OXIDATIVE LEACHING.
ATMOSPHERIC PRESSURE LEACHING.REAGENTS RECOVERY//
NITRIC ACID

LVF 5.652 WEAR-RESISTANT ANODIC COATING FOR TITANIUM.
           CHEVALIER,J.;MOISAN,J.;MOLINIER,R..MET.FINISH
           ,J..1971.DEC..P.313 (3P).(ELECTROMET.)
PRODUCTION AND PROPERTIES OF AN ANODIC COATING ON TI-6A
1-4V ALLOY.
KEYWORDS: ANODES.COATINGS.TITANIUM.WEAR.ALLOYS.
CORROSION//ANODIC OXIDATION

LVF 5.653 POTENTIAL APPLICATION OF NOVEL ROCK DISINTEGR
           ATION TECHNIQUES IN MINING. MAURER,W.C.;31ST
           .ANNU.MIN.SYP.;& 43RD.ANNU.MEET..MINNESOTA SEC
           T..1970.JAN.,P.87 (18P).(CHEM ENG.)
KEYWORDS: ROCK DISINTEGRATION.LASERS.ELECTRON BEAMS.
EROSION DRILLS.THERMAL COMMINUTION.SPALLING.DRILLING.
ROCK BREAKAGE

LVF 5.654 THE PRESENT STATE OF SCALE CONTROL IN SEA WAT
           ER EVAPORATORS. ELLIOT,M.N..DESALINATION.196
           9.6. P.87 (18P).(CHEM. ENG.)
PRESENT METHODS OF SCALE CONTROL AND PROPOSED ALTERNATI
VES ARE DISCUSSED.

KEYWORDS: DESALINATION.SCALE DEPOSITS.SOLUBILITY.
HEAT TRANSFER.PH ADJUSTMENT/CALCIUM SULFATE.
CALCIUM CARBONATE.MAGNESIUM HYDROXIDE

LVF 5.655 BEHAVIOR, PROPERTIES AND PREPARATION OF MnO_2
           ANODES.BIBLIOGRAPHY. GAGNE,F.;CRANE,M.;(INC
           O).JRGRL BIBLIOGR..1972.DEC.05.(8P).(ELECTROME
           T.)
KEYWORDS: ANODES//BIBLIOGRAPHY (JRGRL)
MANGANESE DIOXIDE

LVF 5.656 ROLE OF THE CATHODIC GENERATION OF HYDROGEN D
           URING THE FORMATION OF NICKEL COATINGS. BERE
           ZINA,S.T.;GORBACHUK,G.A.;KUREIKOVA,A.N..ELEKTR
           OKHIMIYA.1971.7(4). P.467 (7P).(RUSS).(ELECTRO
           CE)
KEYWORDS: NICKEL.ELECTRODEPOSITION.HYDROGEN.COATINGS

LVF 5.657 INFLUENCE OF TEMPERATURE AND MOISTURE ON CORR
           OSION OF METALS IN AN ATMOSPHERE OF SULFUR DIO
           XIDE. PRYOR,M.;.APPL.CHEM.//
           USSR..1948.21(4). P.362 (10P).(RUSS).(MAINTENAN
           CE)
KEYWORDS: CORROSION-SULFUR DICXIDE.
TEMPERATURE DEPENDENCE//STEEL.MOISTURE DEPENDENCE

LVF 5.658 THE BOTTOM-BLOWN OXYGEN CONVERTER. A NEW METH
           OD OF STEELMAKING. BROTZMANN,K.;TECH.FORSCH.
           .1968.NO.172(41). P.718 (3P).(PYROMET.)
INF.TRANS: 1969/722 (BISI 7255).
KEYWORDS: CONVERTERS.NOZZLES.IMPURITIES REMOVAL//
BOTTOM-BLOWN OXYGEN CONVERTERS.DEPHOSPHORIZATION.STEEL

LVF 5.659 THE PRESENT STATE AND TRENDS OF THE PELLETIZI
           NG PROCESS. JERNKONTORETS ANN..1
           971.155(5).733 (18P).(SWED)
DISCUSSION OF METHODS AND EQUIPMENT.
KEYWORDS: PELLETIZING//GREEN PELLETS

LVF 5.660 THE $CoCl_2$-$FeCl_2$-H_2O SYSTEM AT 60 DEGREES C.
           SHCHEDRINA,A.P.;KRASNOVA,L.N..MELINICHENKO,L.
           M..RUSS.J.INORG.CHEM..(ENGL.TRANSL.).1971.16(1
           2). P.1744 (2P).(PHYS.CHEM. DATA)
KEYWORDS: SOLUBILITY.CHLORIDES/SOLID SOLUTIONS.
SYSTEM.$CoCl_2$-$FeCl_2$-H_2O.PHASE COMPOSITION

LVF 5.661 THE $CuSO_4$-$(NH_4)_2SO_4$-H_2O SYSTEM AT 40 DEGREES
           C. AKBAEV,A.;EZHOVA,V.V.;PAMATKANOVA,A..RUSS.
           J.INORG.CHEM.(ENGL.TRANSL.).1971.16(15). P.16A
           2 (2P).(PHYS.CHEM. DATA.HYDROCMET.)

Figure 19: Extract from bibliographic listing, International Nickel Company of Canada Limited

VERTICAL FILE: 5466-6765: KEYWORDS

BRAZIL
PLATINIFFERROUS CHROMITITE IN THE TOCANTINS COMPL
EX NIQUELANDIA, GOIAS, BRAZIL. (1971).....LVF 5,780

BIBLIOGRAPHY ON GEOLOGY AND MINERALOGY IN BRAZI
L. (1973,JUL.).....LVF 6,326

BREAKAGE FUNCTIONS
A COMBINED TRACER AND BACK-CALCULATION METHOD F
OR DETERMINING PARTICULATE BREAKAGE FUNCTIONS I
N BALL MILLING. PART I: RATIONALE AND DESCRIPTI
ON OF THE PROPOSED METHOD. (1972).....LVF 5,642

A COMBINED TRACER AND BACK-CALCULATION METHOD F
OR DETERMINING PARTICULATE BREAKAGE FUNCTIONS I
N BALL MILLING. PART II: APPLICATION TO HEMATIT
E IRON ORE IN A BATCH LABORATORY. (1972).....LVF 5,643

BRECCIA
ROLE OF THIOBACILLUS FERROOXIDANS IN LEACHING U
F NI, CU, CO, FE, AL, AND CA FROM ORES OF COPPE
R-NICKEL DEPOSITS. (1971).....LVF 5,617

BRICKS
INFLUENCING THE SERVICE LIFE OF BASIC CONVERTER
LININGS FOR THE TOP-BLOWING OXYGEN PROCESS (1
973,APR.).....LVF 6,583

BASIC REFRACTORIES IN ELECTRIC ARC SIDEWALLS (1
973).....LVF 6,676

BRIGHTENERS
SELECTION OF AN ELECTROLYTE FOR BRIGHT NICKEL P
LATING. (1971).....LVF 5,718

ANIONIC IMPURITIES IN ELECTRODEPOSITED COPPER.
(1972).....LVF 6,030

USE AND EFFECT OF GLYCFODORIC ACID IN BRIGHT-N
ICKEL ELECTROLYTES. (1972).....LVF 6,054

BRIGHTENING AGENTS
BRIGHTENING AND LEVELING AGENTS IN NICKEL ELECT
ROPLATING. BIBLIOGRAPHY. (1974,FEB.).....LVF 6,668

BRITISH COLUMBIA
BACKGROUND DATA FOR BIOGEOCHEMICAL PROSPECTING
IN BRITISH COLUMBIA (1962,JUN.).....LVF 5,504

SOME CHEMICAL CHARACTERISTICS OF THE INTRUSIVE
ROCKS OF THE BETHLEHEM PORPHYRY COPPER DEPOSITS
, B.C. (1971,OCT.).....LVF 6,006

THE OLD NICK PROSPECT - A NICKEL DEPOSIT IN SOU
THERN BRITISH COLUMBIA. (1971,FEB.).....LVF 6,221

BRITTLENESS
ELECTROLYTIC EVOLUTION OF GAS. (1972).....LVF 5,619

BRIKLEGG ELECTRIC-SMELTING PROC
BRIKLEGG ELECTRIC SMELTING PROCESS APPLIED T
O COPPER CONCENTRATES (1972).....LVF 6,764

BROMINE
MASS-SPECTROMETRIC INVESTIGATION OF THE NICKEL-
BROMINE SURFACE REACTION. (1964,JAN.).....LVF 5,866

BRUCITE
THE CRYSTALLIZATION OF MAGNESIUM HYDROXIDE. (19
73).....LVF 6,211

ARTIFICIAL CONVERSION OF OLIVINE INTO A SERPENT
INE MINERAL. (1969).....LVF 6,217

BUBBLE ATTACHMENT
AN INSTRUMENT FOR MEASURING THE ADHESION TIME O
F GAS BUBBLES TO MINERAL PARTICLES IN ELECTROFL
OTATION. (1971).....LVF 6,276

BUBBLE FORMATION
RATE OF FLOW AND MECHANICS OF BUBBLE FORMATION
FROM SINGLE SUBMERGED ORIFICES. (1956,SEP.).....LVF 6,359

BUBBLES
ELECTROLYTIC EVOLUTION OF GAS. (1972).....LVF 5,619

THE ADSORPTION OF SODIUM LAURYL SULFATE AND LAU
RYL ALCOHOL AT THE AIR-LIQUID INTERFACE. (1957).....LVF 5,629

AN IMPROVED APPARATUS FOR THE STUDY OF FOAMS. (
1962,NOV.).....LVF 5,630

STABILITY CRITERION OF FOAMS AND METHODS FOR IT
S DETERMINATION. (1971).....LVF 5,887

AN INSTRUMENT FOR MEASURING THE ADHESION TIME O
F GAS BUBBLES TO MINERAL PARTICLES IN ELECTROFL
OTATION. (1971).....LVF 6,276

RATE OF FLOW AND MECHANICS OF BUBBLE FORMATION
FROM SINGLE SUBMERGED ORIFICES. (1956,SEP.).....LVF 6,359

THE MECHANISMS BY WHICH PARTICLES SEGREGATE IN
GAS FLUIDISED BEDS BINARY SYSTEMS OF NEAR-SPHE
RICAL PARTICLES. (1972).....LVF 6,434

ENERGY REQUIREMENTS FOR MIXING. BIBLIOGRAPHY. (
1974,JAN.).....LVF 6,625

PHYSICAL RATE PROCESSES IN INDUSTRIAL FERMENTAT
ION. PART I: THE INTERFACIAL AREA IN GAS-LIQUID
CONTACTING WITH MECHANICAL AGITATION. (1958).....LVF 6,680

Figure 20: Extract from basic keyword index, International Nickel Company of Canada Limited

Canada.[24] (Ms Campey also provides useful information about other kinds of computer-generated indexes including citation indexes, book catalogues, SLIC indexes, articulated subject indexes and post-co-ordinate indexes.) More recently KWIC and KWOC indexes have been produced by other kinds of libraries, an example being Glasgow University library's *KWIC index to general reference books in Glasgow University library* (rev ed 1976).

The University of Bath maintains a KWOC index as well as a more conventional classified catalogue and chain index. There is very little enrichment of titles, apart from the use of secondary titles and some corporate authors, conference headings and place information. The students make heavy use of this index. Needham has reported that thirty-one per cent of the participants in a survey used the KWOC index as their first choice when carrying out searches, compared with four per cent who chose the classified catalogue and subject index.[25] Success rates were also higher with the KWOC index.

The KWOC index, which is very elementary, was designed in the first instance as an enhanced title catalogue but its potential as a supplementary subject approach was quickly appreciated. Further research commenced at Bath in September 1977 into the problems of subject access to library catalogues through the use of keyword indexes.

The alphabetical section of Liverpool Polytechnic's catalogue includes, as well as entries under authors and series, entries under keywords in titles. For example, *Women and work: sex differences and society* appears under SEX DIFFERENCES, SOCIETY, WOMEN and WORK.

Elizabeth Al-Hazzam has described a KWOC index introduced in 1972 to provide multiple access points to the map collection of Arizona State University's Hayden Library.[26] This index is based not on titles but on a thesaurus which includes some Library of Congress subject headings but consists mainly of terms from class G of the Library of Congress Classification and from information on the face of maps in the collection. Standard abbreviations are used for the names of states and for well-known terminology as subheadings, as in the following examples:

ARIZONA – NATL FORESTS
NATIONAL FORESTS – ARIZ

There is an abbreviations file, and abbreviations are also noted on cards in the thesaurus file.

REFERENCES

1 Notably Mills, J 'Chain indexing and the classified catalogue' *Library Association record* 57(4) April 1955, 141-148; also the same author's 'Indexing a classification scheme' *The indexer* 2(2) autumn 1960, 40-48.

2 Hicks, Suzanne C 'A defence of chain indexing' *Australian library journal* 21(9) October 1972, 373-375.

3 Armsby, A F 'Information retrieval: a method for school libraries' *School librarian* 22(3) September 1974, 224-228.

4 Library of Congress. Subject Cataloging Division. *Subject headings used in the dictionary catalogs of the Library of Congress* 8th ed. Washington, 1976. 2 vols.

5 Kanwischer, Dorothy 'Subject headings trauma: making do with first aid' *Wilson library bulletin* 49(9) May 1975, 651-654.

6 Hazen, Margaret Hindle 'The closing of the classified catalog at Boston University' *Library resources and technical services* 18(3) summer 1974, 220-225.

7 Enyingi, Peter 'Subject cataloging practices in American law libraries' *Law library journal* 68(1) February 1975, 11-17.

8 *Medical subject headings* Bethesda, Maryland, National Library of Medicine, annual. 2 vols.

9 McNutt, Eleanor M and Poland, Ursula H 'Three-way catalog division combined with conversion to *Medical subject headings* (MeSH) in a medium-sized medical library' *Bulletin of the Medical Library Association* 62(4) October 1974, 388-396.

10 Charen, Thelma *MEDLARS indexing manual* Washington, US Government Printing Office for the National Library of Medicine, 1969.

11 McGlynn, Shirley 'The School of Public Health and Tropical Medicine library, Sydney' *Australian special library news* 8(1) March 1975, 20-27.

12 Caspari, Sarah B and Batty, Ellen L 'A description of the catalog division project at the College of Physicians of Philadelphia library' *Bulletin of the Medical Library Association* 63(3) July 1975, 302-308.

13 Coates, E J *Subject catalogues: headings and structure*. London, Library Association, 1960.

14 Gould, Angela M 'User preference in published indexes' *Journal of the American Society for Information Science* 25(5) September-October 1974, 279-286.

15 Cornwall, G St C, Jones, K P and Pattin, A M *'British technology index* as a basis for the subject catalogue' *Catalogue and index* (12) October 1968, 8-10.

16 Personal communication from Kevin Jones

17 Notably Austin, Derek *PRECIS: a manual of concept analysis and subject indexing* London, Council of the British National Bibliography, 1974. Other contributions include the same author's 'The development of PRECIS: a theoretical and technical history' *Journal of documentation* 30(1) March 1974,

47-102; Bakewell, K G B 'The PRECIS indexing system' *The indexer* 9(4) October 1975, 160-166.

18 Lynch, Michael F 'Computer-organised display of subject information' *The indexer* 7(3) spring 1971, 94-100.

19 Lynch, M F and Petrie, J H 'A program suite for the production of articulated subject indexes' *Computer journal* 16(1) February 1973, 46-57.

20 Belton, M 'Computer-aided production of the subject index to the SMRE Bibliography' *The indexer* 8(1) April 1972, 44-49.

21 Sharp, John R *Some fundamentals of information retrieval* London, Deutsch, 1965.

22 Luhn, H P *Keyword in context index for technical literature* New York, IBM, 1959.

23 Flury, William R and Henderson, Diane D 'A user oriented KWIC index: KWOC-ed, tagged and enriched' (in American Society for Information Science 33rd annual meeting, October 11-15, 1970. *Proceedings vol 7: The information conscious society* (ed) Jeanne B North. Washington (DC), 1970, pp 101-105).

24 Campey, Lucille H *Generating and printing indexes by computer* London, Aslib, 1972. (occasional publication no 11). Updated in Campey, Lucille H 'Generating and printing indexes by computer' *Program* 8(3) July 1974, 149-165.

25 Needham, Angela *Performance of four orders of catalogue: user times and success rates for name, title, KWOC and classified catalogues* and *Classified or KWOC catalogues: an indicative comparison of the success and usability of a KWOC catalogue with UDC catalogues at four university libraries* Bath, Bath University Library, 1975 (Bath University comparative catalogue study: final report, paper nos 5 and 6, bound together).

26 Al-Hazzam, Elizabeth, Arizona State University, Hayden Library, 'KWOC index to the map collection' *Western Association of Map Libraries information bulletin* 5(1) November 1973, 26-37.

169

Chapter Eight

THE ALPHABETICAL SUBJECT APPROACH
POST-CO-ORDINATE

POST-CO-ORDINATE INDEXING, whereby the combination of concepts in a compound subject is done at the time of search rather than at the time of indexing, has rapidly gained ground in special libraries since the introduction by Mortimer Taube of the uniterm system in 1953.[1] Taube's system consisted of giving each document a number and entering this number on to cards which had been specially ruled into ten columns and which bore the appropriate subject terms as headings. For example, a document on ergonomics and aircraft accidents might be given the number 253 which would then be entered (posted) on cards headed ACCIDENTS, AIRCRAFT and ERGONO-MICS. The number is normally entered in the column of the card corresponding to its final digit (a system known as terminal digit posting), so that 253 would be entered in the third column. This makes it easier to read off the numbers when comparing several cards to locate documents on complex subjects.

Since Taube's original uniterm cards there have been a number of developments including the use of edge-notched cards and the very popular punched feature cards, also called optical coincidence or OCCI cards (see figure twenty-one, page 175). Campbell has provided useful information about 146 post-co-ordinate indexes in Britain alone[2], and he admits that there may be many more unknown to him. A system at the British Standards Institution's Technical Help for Exporters, using Thesaurofacet for vocabulary control, was described in chapter six. In recent years, as indicated in Beswick's final report for the Schools Council's Resource Centres project,[3] such systems have been widely used in British school libraries and resource centres.

Codsall High School, near Wolverhampton

Beswick tends to sit on the fence with regard to information retrieval systems but appears to distrust OCCI and states that the case for it was 'judged not proven.'[4] Be that as it may, the system works very well for non-book materials at Codsall High School, and the teacher-librarian suggested to me one very good reason for its use in addition to its efficiency: pupils enjoy using feature cards but are generally unhappy using conventional card catalogues.

At the time of the Beswick study, books were classified by DC *and* included in the OCCI system, which seemed unnecessary duplication. They are now only included in the OCCI system if the Dewey number is not an obvious one or if detailed analysis is required. For example Sheila Gordon's *World problems* (Batsford, 1971) can only be classified at 301 (Sociology), but a major section of the book dealing with violence and the use of force can be indexed on an OCCI card under VIOLENCE, thus avoiding the need for analytical entries (for which there would probably not be time anyway).

Many librarians, including Beswick, regard the possibility of 'false drops' (such as the retrieval of an item on exports from the USA to Britain when one really wants something on exports from Britain to the USA) as a major problem of post-co-ordinate indexing. Codsall does not, however, find this a particular difficulty. On the other hand, a point which Beswick does not regard as serious—the difficulty of 'unpunching' a hole when an item is withdrawn—is regarded as more serious by Codsall.

The following extracts from an excellent guide given to pupils demonstrate very well how the Codsall system works:

NON-BOOK MATERIAL

The library stores more than just books. In the Resource Centre storeroom we keep filmstrips, tapes and records. Filmstrips and tapes can be used in the library using the tape recorder and filmstrip viewers provided. To find out what we have stored we have a second system to use alongside the Dewey system. It is called OCCI. These letters stand for Optical Coincidence Card Index.

As you enter the library you will see two metal boxes with large cards in them. These are OCCI boxes. All the cards in the boxes are labelled and the boxes are divided down into different sections. These are:

1 Who is it for?
2 What is it for?
3 What period of time is it about?
4 What school subject is it about?
5 What place is it about?
6 What topic or theme is it about?

When you are looking for material you must follow this process:

1 Decide which of the cards to choose. First take out your year card. If you are a third year take out the third year card as this will stop you finding material that was meant for sixth formers that will be too difficult for you at the moment. Then choose your other cards —eg if you are from IDE working on animals you will choose these cards.

2 Put the cards together very accurately and place them on the light box. Switch the light on and you will see that the light will shine through some holes in the cards. To find out the number of the hole read the large red letters first and then the small black letters. Make a note of the numbers in your rough book. If no light shines through, it means we have no material stored in the OCCI box about that subject but don't forget to look for any books using the Dewey system.

3 If you have chosen the cards out of the OCCI box marked 'A numbers', you must look these up in the catalogue drawers marked 'OCCI box A numbers'. If you have chosen your cards from the other box, you look up these in the catalogue drawers marked ACCESSION. Look up the number and the card will tell you what the item is and what it is about. If it is a book the card will tell you its name, author and Dewey number:

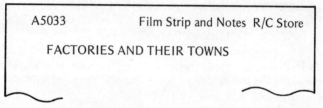

```
A5660                    R P A Edwards

301                      THE TOWER BLOCK
```

You then find the book on the Dewey shelf.

If it is not a book the card will tell you what it is and where it is stored:

```
A5033              Film Strip and Notes  R/C Store

       FACTORIES AND THEIR TOWNS
```

You must then ask the teacher on duty if you may have the item and she will get it for you.

Pink cards mean filmstrips or slides; yellow cards mean tapes or records; white cards mean books.

The following notes amplify some of the above points:

Who is is for? There are only six feature cards in this group: third year, fourth year, fifth year CSE, fifth year O level, sixth form, staff.

What is it? This represents the form of the item (eg book, tape, record, filmstrip). Obviously, these cards will not be consulted unless the enquirer is *only* interested in a particular medium.

What period of time is it about? Those covered are: before 500 BC; 5000-2500 BC; 2500-500 BC; 500-250 BC; 250 BC-250 AD; 250-1000 AD;

1000-1250 AD; 1250-1500 AD; 1500-1600 AD; 1600-1700 AD; 1700-1800 AD; 1800-1850 AD; 1850-1900 AD; 1900-1925 AD; 1925-1950 AD; 1950-1960 AD; 1960-1970 AD; since 1970; the future.

What school subject is it about? This section contains thirty-eight cards representing the broad subject areas of the school curriculum (eg art, community studies, environmental studies, geography, Russian, woodwork).

What place is it about? The breakdown here is mainly by continent apart from cards for local, East Anglia, England, Great Britain, Scotland, Wales, Ireland, Northern Ireland, India, China, Japan, space, fictional places and the world.

What topic or theme is it about? In 1976 there were approximately 350 headings or 'features', with a marked bias towards the humanities —a contrast from the scientific and technical environment in which post-co-ordinate indexing was first introduced.

The 'features' within the broad groups (audience, item, period, school subject, place, theme) are typed on different coloured cards to obviate the possibility of filing errors. The reason for two OCCI boxes is simply that all 10,000 holes were punched in the first box. This is another reason for the decision to index books selectively.

Hazel Grove High School, Stockport

In the Resources Centre at Hazel Grove High School·a different indexing system is used from that for books and the stock is not therefore completely integrated. Largely influenced by the experiences of Codsall, it was decided to use post-co-ordinate indexing or OCCI for the audio-visual materials in the resources centre.

The present librarian, Mrs P Tidy, has reservations about the system and thinks there would be advantages in using Dewey throughout with an integrated classified catalogue. One very practical advantage of OCCI, however, is that teachers can do their own indexing, which they might find difficult using DC as well as producing inconsistencies. The following note is given to teachers to help them in indexing:

INSTRUCTIONS FOR FEATURING

Please underline the features listed below which are applicable to your item.

When indexing the subject content of your document remember that it is only necessary to indicate those topics which are significantly represented. If the less important aspects of the item are indexed it may result in material which is of little relevance being retrieved.

Additional guidance on featuring is given on a separate sheet, together with a thesaurus. Please consult this before featuring.

NB As this is only an interim list topics which you feel should be indexed may not appear. In this case please add such terms as are necessary to describe the content of the item in the space provided at the end of the topic list. In due course these terms, or their equivalents, will be incorporated into the next edition of the list.

Punching of holes on the feature cards is done by volunteer parents, which is another argument in favour of OCCI.

The fact that many enquiries involve only one feature—and very few involve more than three—means that a post-co-ordinate system may not really be necessary. On the other hand the system would cope more satisfactorily than Dewey with some books. For example, reference was made on page 32 to a social survey of Victorian children, classified at 942.081 which does not bring out 'children'. Using the OCCI system, this could be indexed under CHILDREN, SOCIAL, HISTORY, ENGLAND and 1800-1899.

A real problem found with the present use of OCCI is that the feature headings tend to be too general and have not kept pace with curriculum development. For example, an enquiry for information on the reaction of iron and sulphur can only be answered by consulting the card for METALS (see figure twenty-one) and then checking all the appropriate numbers in the card index. As it happens, one of the earliest numbers (1004) deals with this particular subject (a chemistry department worksheet on reacting iron and sulphur) but it could easily have been one of the later numbers and in any case it would be necessary to check each one.

A check of the numbers on the METALS card also brings out an advantage of OCCI: number 1253 is a collection of slides on 'Old industries 1870-1970' which is indexed under each industry. Using conventional classification and cataloguing, this can only be done by making many analytical entries.

It might be argued that the problem of general headings can be overcome by revising the features list, but this is not easily done because of the necessity to check every item indexed. Occasionally new terms have been introduced with a note that more general headings need to be consulted before a particular number.

The features used are divided into the following seven groups:
Location (resources centre; department; person; other)
Form (thirty-four features including diagram, examination paper, game, slide, tape etc)
Date (eighteen features from prehistory to future).
Audience suitability (first year; second year; third year; fourth year; fifth year; sixth year; CSE; O level; A level; remedial; staff).
School subject (thirty-three features).
Place (126 features).
Topics (290 features).

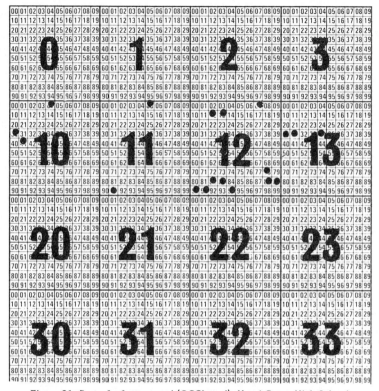

Figure 21: Part of a feature card (OCCI card), Hazel Grove High School. The punched holes indicate that documents with the following numbers deal with the subject of the card (in this case, metals): 1004, 1030, 1041, 1105, 1191, 1207, 1212, 1213, 1253, 1278, 1282, 1283, 1288, 1289, 1290, 1291, 1294, 1330, 1331, 1334.

The full potential of the system is shown in an example included in the *Resources centre handbook*, a copy of which is given to all teaching staff. A pack of slides on the history of commercial aviation would be indexed as follows:

Location:	resources centre
Form:	slides
Date:	1960-1969; since 1970
Audience suitability:	all features
School subject:	general studies; history; general science; technology
Place:	—
Topics:	air; flight; design; communications; transport; history; technology

175

At present there are approximately 3,000 items on the OCCI system, meaning that less than one-third of the 10,000-hole capacity of each card is used.

Although the present librarian has reservations about OCCI and would like an integrated system using Dewey, a glance at the features list shows a number of subjects which it would be difficult to classify satisfactorily by DC such as Authority, Culture, Energy/Power, Environment, Imagination, Protection, Water, and Women.

British Institute of Management

At the British Institute of Management, a post-co-ordinate indexing system has been used, for journal articles only, since 1969. The index now covers approximately 16,000 articles on 10,000-hole feature cards and these are increasing at the rate of 4,000 articles per annum. The thesaurus was originally compiled by the then librarian John Blagden and published as *Management information retrieval: a new indexing language*[5]. Various amendments have been made such as the introduction of the important term MANPOWER PLANNING instead of punching PERSONNEL and PLANNING (an interesting example of increased pre-co-ordination). New terms include

MANAGEMENT THRESHOLD
    punch also CAREER PATTERNS + MANAGEMENT DEVELOP-
    MENT + MANAGERS + MOTIVATION
QUALITY OF WORKING LIFE
    punch also JOB ENRICHMENT + MORALE + PERSONNEL
    MANAGEMENT

In addition to the sequence under subject headings (or keywords), articles are indexed under author and journal title, and there is an entry under accession number which serves as an authority file by listing all the keywords used to index the article, thus:

B004674

Forecasting: prelude to managerial planning
Richard J Tenbine
Managerial planning: July/August 1975, p 11-17, 23
Economics/Multiple Regression Analysis/Statistics/Planning/
Business cycles/Time series/Models (operational research)

ICI Fibres, Harrogate

Post-co-ordinate indexing is used by ICI Fibres for reports, mainly internal, which are arranged in accession number order. There are some interesting differences in the thesauri compiled at Pontypool and Harrogate, the latter containing many more pre-co-ordinate terms. As a simple example, HEAT TRANSFER is used at Harrogate but HEAT + TRANSMISSION are used at Pontypool.

The computer

A great advantage of post-co-ordinate indexing is the ease with which it can be applied to computerized systems by feeding in keywords and letting the computer do the rest. Various organizations, such as Lockheed Information Systems (with its Dialog information retrieval service), the System Development Corporation and Bibliographical Retrieval Service, provide access to a wide variety of data bases.

Judith Yarborough of the ERIC Clearinghouse on Information Resources has provided useful guidance for making a computer search of the ERIC (Educational Resources Information Center) data base. First one should decide whether a computer search or a manual one is more appropriate and then whether it should be retrospective, specific query or current awareness. The problem should be defined and the search strategy evolved. The keywords may then be fed into the computer: these may be authors, institutions, descriptors from the ERIC thesaurus[7] and 'identifiers' (ie terms which reflect the content of a document but are not in the ERIC thesaurus, such as people, places, trade names and names of projects). Descriptors from the ERIC thesaurus may be classified into four groups: population (eg occupation, age, race, physical characteristics); action or material concepts; curriculum concepts; and document form or type concepts.

A survey in spring 1973 provided information about the reactions of 141 users to the PROBE computer retrieval program, developed at Indiana University by Ronald Tschudi using the ERIC data base.[8] Asked to grade the information they received, the users gave the following answers:

very high value	27.8 per cent
high value	34.5 per cent
medium value	17.2 per cent
little value	10.6 per cent
no value	9.9 per cent

MEDLINE was begun by the National Library of Medicine in October 1971 as an on-line offshoot of its earlier MEDLARS (Medical Literature Analysis and Retrieval System), using the MeSH list (referred to in chapter seven) as its index language. There has been an interesting case study of its use in Tufts University Medical and Dental Library, which serves a rapidly expanding medical and dental complex in Boston's downtown area.[9] Tufts began subscribing to MEDLINE in March 1972 and its popularity is shown by the increase in the number of searches since that date. The need to use MEDLINE terminology in searches is seen as a major problem, but it is suggested that 'the ever increasing use of the MEDLINE system at Tufts demonstrates that users will work through difficulties of the man-machine interface and

177

the frustration of handling a preconstructed vocabulary if the retrieval of citations is fast, accurate and free of charge' (which it is at Tufts for persons associated with the school though a charge of $10 per search is made for unaffiliated persons). However it is pointed out that it will be many years before the MEDLINE service becomes a complete bibliographical service as many sources in the medical and scientific literature are not included in *Index medicus* and are therefore not covered in MEDLINE.

There have been several studies of reactions to MEDLINE, one of the most useful being Renata Tagliacozzo's survey of 810 users in seven US centres—the University of Illinois at the Medical Center, Chicago; Indiana University School of Medicine; the University of Chicago; the University of Illinois at Urbana; Cleveland Health Services Library; the Mayo Clinic; and Wayne State University.[10] There were 1047 completed questionnaires, 93.6 per cent of which came from the first four centres mentioned. Reasons quoted for requesting a MEDLINE search included: obtaining references that might have been missed (863 respondents); saving time and/or effort (845); uncovering obscure references (642); wanting to get acquainted with new fields (334) and gaining a feeling of security (143). It was found that users of MEDLINE tended to be academics involved in research in basic as well as clinical sciences and/or students working for higher degrees or in clinical training.

A questionnaire survey by the Louis Calder Memorial Library of the University of Miami School of Medicine showed that sixty-two per cent of the 264 respondents received about the right number of citations, 16.7 per cent received too few citations and 17.3 per cent received too many irrelevant citations.[11]

A comparison of manual and MEDLINE literature searches at the Northwestern and Fairview Hospitals, Minneapolis, showed that in all but two cases MEDLINE bibliographies included relevant citations not retrieved manually.[12] Forty-three per cent of the respondents considered the MEDLINE searches excellent, thirty-six per cent satisfactory and twenty-one per cent poor. Forty-five per cent found the manual search completely satisfactory, thirty-eight per cent partially satisfactory and seventeen per cent unsatisfactory.

The Kresge Library of Oakland University, Rochester, Michigan, has no school of medicine but supports graduate programmes in psychology, biology, engineering, education and physics. Thirty-six searches were generated by twenty-one staff and students through the library between January and April 1974, the average search taking thirty-two minutes of terminal contact time and requiring twenty-five linkages by Boolean algebra. Twenty-seven evaluations were returned, and these indicated that twenty-five of the searches were of major value

178

to the user and two of minor value. All the searchers found the title to be of major value as a citation component and sixty-seven per cent considered the subject heading to be of considerable importance. The average precision value for the twenty-seven searches evaluated was 53.9 per cent. All users expressed willingness to pay for future searches, suggested amounts ranging between two and fifty dollars. The general conclusion is that 'in regard to user satisfaction MEDLINE can operate at least as effectively in the academic sector as in a medical or clinical situation.'[13]

Commenting on the use of MEDLINE on a trial basis at Poole General Hospital, Carmel states that, while the system has been 'occasionally disappointing and frequently frustrating,' its successes have been 'often very useful and occasionally quite spectacular.'[14] S J Pritchard, after describing the use of MEDLINE in the Welsh National School of Medicine Library in the University Hospital of Wales, sees it as 'a developing system with . . . an impressive record of increasing sophistication and flexibility.'[15]

Cost data at Central Research, Pfizer Inc, Groton, Connecticut, has shown that MEDLINE searching is superior in quality to manual searching of *Index medicus* but that on-line searching of *Chemical abstracts* keywords is not an effective substitute for manual searching of *Chemical abstracts* substance indexes.[16]

A questionnaire survey of one hundred US academic libraries with separate departmental chemistry or science libraries to explore their use of on-line computer-based bibliographical searches had a seventy-three per cent response rate, of which 49.3 per cent were using such services and 24.6 per cent were planning to use them.[17] The searches met the needs of the users 'most of the time' in 83.3 per cent of the organizations and 'all the time' in 5.4 per cent. Two or more services were used in 72.2 per cent of the organizations and a single service in the others, the most popular services being MEDLINE, Lockheed, and the System Development Corporation.

Finally a very useful survey at North Carolina Science and Technology Research Center of the cost of computer searches of fifteen services concludes with the suggestion that there will be a move towards automatic indexing by computer in the form of full-text searching of abstracts in the whole document because of the increasing cost of manual indexing and the difficulty of obtaining qualified indexers.[18]

References
1 Taube, Mortimer and associates *Studies in co-ordinate indexing* Washington (DC), Documentation Inc, 1953.
2 Campbell, D J *A survey of British practice in co-ordinate indexing in information/library units* London, Aslib, 1975.

3 Beswick, Norman *Organising resources: six case studies: the final report of the Schools Council Resource Centre Project* London, Heinemann Educational, 1975.

4 Ibid, p 80.

5 Blagden, John F *Management information retrieval: a new indexing language* 2nd ed. London, Management publications, 1971.

6 Yarborough, Judith 'How to prepare for a computer search of ERIC: a non-technical approach' *Information reports and bibliographies* 4(5) 1975, 13-23.

7 Educational Resources Information Center *Thesaurus of ERIC descriptors* 6th ed New York, Macmillan Information; London, Collier Macmillan, 1975.

8 Kiewitt, Eva L 'A user study of a computer retrieval system' *College and research libraries* 36(6) November 1975, 458-463.

9 'Tufts University Medical and Dental Library MEDLINE system' (in Palmer, Richard Philips (ed) *Case studies in library computer systems* New York, Bowker, 1973.

10 Tagliacozzo, Renata 'The consumers of new information technology: a survey of the utilization of MEDLINE' *Journal of the American Society for Information Science* 26(5) September-October 1975, 294-304.

11 McCarthy, Susan E, Maccabee, Shirley S and Feng, Cyril C H 'Evaluation of MEDLINE services by user survey' *Bulletin of the Medical Library Association* 62(4) October 1974, 367-373.

12 Foreman, Gertrude, Allen, Margaret and Johnson, Donna 'A user study of manual and MEDLINE literature searches in the hospital library' *Bulletin of the Medical Library Association* 62(4) October 1974, 385-387.

13 Hitchingham, Eileen E 'MEDLINE use in a university without a school of medicine' *Special libraries* 67(4) April 1976, 188-194.

14 Carmel, M J 'MEDLINE in a hospital library' *Library Association Medical Section bulletin* (101) May 1975, 4-6.

15 Pritchard, S J 'MEDLINE in a medical school library' *Library Association Medical Section bulletin* (103) November 1975, 5-7.

16 Buckley, Jay S 'Planning for effective use of on-line systems' *Journal of chemical information and computer sciences* 15(3) August 1975, 161-164.

17 Marshall, Doris B: A survey of the use of on-line computer-based scientific search services by academic libraries *Journal of chemical information and computer sciences* 15(4) November 1975, 247-249.

18 Cheney, Peter J 'Cost of computer searching' *RQ* 12(3) spring 1973, 251-258.

Chapter Nine

RECLASSIFICATION

EVEN THE PUBLICATION of a new edition of a particular classification scheme can involve libraries in a large amount of reclassification,
and the situation is a good deal worse if the change is from one scheme
to another. That this is not an unusual occurrence will be obvious from
the preceding chapters.

First the librarian will have to convince his superiors (eg local
authority, university court, polytechnic academic board, headmaster,
senior manager etc) that the exercise is worthwhile—ie that there is
a good reason for reclassifying. If the change is to DC or LC it may be
possible to point to the expected advantages from increased use of
centralized services. Administrative convenience may indeed be the
only reason for change. The Baker Library of Harvard University
Graduate School of Business Administration changed in 1976 from a
very effective special scheme tailor-made to its own requirements[1] to
LC in order to make full use of network capabilities.[2]

The change may be forced by the merger of two libraries using
different classification schemes, as happened to the libraries of two
British government departments—the Ministry of Transport and the
Ministry of Housing and Local Government—on the formation of the
Department of the Environment in 1970.

If the change is made because of anticipated benefits in terms of
improved reader services—perhaps the revised BC or one of the special
schemes is being adopted—then in theory it may be possible to use a
cost-benefit approach to justify the change by calculating the amount
of time likely to be saved on enquiry work following the use of a more
effective classification. In practice, of course, this might prove a very
difficult exercise.

Johnson has demonstrated the value of a management by objectives
approach in his account of the reclassification of Pennsylvania State
University from DC to LC.[3] The four major steps are:

1 analyse the amount of material needing reclassification;
2 set the objectives in terms of quantitative and qualitative goals
   for a given period of time;
3 set target dates; and

4 identify any obstacles to the achievement of these targets and
   remove them.

Reclassification can be avoided by simply starting to use the new classification for all stock added after a certain date, leaving earlier material as it is. The problem then is that there will always be two sequences to consult unless enquiries have a cut-off date later than the date of new classification. The Baker Library at Harvard Business School only reclassified its post-1970 acquisitions of books and pamphlets but it also reclassified its complete reference collection, its core collection of about 4,000 recent business books, and it declassified all serials and periodicals.

Not all material may need reclassification. It may be decided that, applying Ranganathan's 'osmosis' principle, some material can be relegated to reserve stock, retaining its old class number until withdrawn. Other items may be withdrawn at once, thus demonstrating one advantage of reclassification: the opportunity which it affords for stock revision and removal of deadwood as well as for revision of catalogue records. When the libraries of the Ministry of Housing and Local Government and the Ministry of Transport merged, LC was adopted rather than UDC partly because this would involve less reclassification. UDC sections of particular interest to the library, such as traffic engineering, were reclassified immediately but some older and less used material was not reclassified and there remain eighteen drawers of a UDC-based classified catalogue with seven drawers of subject index. A similar procedure will be adopted by the Department of Health and Social Security Library, which expects to adopt some, if not all, of the revised BC schedules. There will, therefore, be a separate sequence of old stock for some time, some of which will eventually be withdrawn and some of which may be reclassified and absorbed into the new stock.

Reclassification will normally be done in sections, either following the sequence of the old or new notation or adopting some other method such as most used section first, most troublesome section first, least troublesome first (since it will be done more quickly) or worst classified section first. The City University, London, reclassifying from UDC to DC, chose to tackle first the area representing the greatest difference of opinion between the two schemes—computer systems, classified at 681.3 in UDC and 001.64 in DC. This also happened to be one of the most popular subjects in the library and so fitted in with the 'most used section first' idea too. It also linked with the library's policy of shelving the DC and UDC classifications in one sequence because of the similarity of their notations, which had many advantages but some disadvantages such as the occasional separation of books on the same subject at two almost adjacent class numbers (eg Electronics, 621.381 in DC and 621.39 in UDC).

Who will do the reclassification? There may be a reclassification team as at the Department of the Environment where two cataloguers worked almost entirely on reclassification for about eighteen months, supported by occasional help from colleagues. In larger libraries it may be possible to second people from other departments to help with the reclassification, and this is likely to be advantageous to the reclassification team (in providing specialist subject advice) and to the seconded personnel (in providing useful cataloguing and classification experience). Schriefer and Atkins have described how 61,803 volumes in the University of California's Law School library were reclassified to LC (and to some extent recatalogued according to AACR) in four months by a team consisting of a project supervisor and nine full-time staff, including four non-cataloguing staff seconded from other departments. [4]

The smaller library may not be able to employ a special team on reclassification. The reclassification of the Library Association library (now the British Library (Library Association Library)) from the sixteenth edition of DC to the preliminary edition of the Classification Research Group Classification of Library Science, which began in 1966, was restricted to current intake, partly because no extra staff were available and partly because a definitve edition was awaited. In September 1974 work began on another reclassification exercise, this time from the CRG scheme to DC18. In fact, apart from an initial reclasification of eighty items from the 1974 and 1975 UK MARC records in order to provide sufficient material for a microfiche catalogue to be produced from MARC records, only multi-volumed works are being reclassified at present. It has been estimated that it would take one person, doing nothing but reclassification, approximately six to seven years to complete the job; as there is no prospect of help for the one full-time cataloguer, reclassification is likely to take a back seat for some time.

It may be possible to use student help, especially during vacations. In an unpublished paper given at Liverpool Polytechnic in 1971, Peter Butcher stated that four second-year students of librarianship from the Polytechnic of North London reclassified the whole of The City University's mathematics section and reached a high level of accuracy, but he pointed out that this might not be the case in more difficult areas or where the classification schedules are less well structured. The reclassification of the University of Southampton's Wessex Medical Library began as an ad hoc operation, with members of staff reclassifying as and when time permitted, but this did not allow satisfactory progress and so special student help was employed during the summer vacation.

In Peter Butcher's paper, the advantages of computerising before reclassifying were stressed, and in particular the ease with which the

184

computer would allow record amendments to be made: apart from the immense saving in routine clerical effort there is, as he pointed out, a saving in professional staff time which might otherwise be spent on proofreading and checking filing. Wassom, Custead and Chen have described the reclassification of 250,000 volumes from DC to LC in seven months using an IBM360/40 computer on-line with an IBM Administrative Terminal System (ATS)/360.[5]

It is an obvious point, but the need to alter *all* records should not be overlooked. Libraries using manual systems should not find it necessary to retype their cards unless they are in a particularly dilapidated condition or the opportunity is being taken to revise cataloguing as well as classification.

Readers may not appreciate the value of reclassification until the exercise is completed, if then, so as little inconvenience as possible should be caused. Certainly the temptation to close the library for reclassification should be resisted, and it may not even be necessary to stop items in the issue and call them in for reclassification: they can be 'trapped' when finally returned. In an academic library it might be possible to attempt most of the reclassification during vacations.

There is no shortage of literature on reclassification, and some years ago Perreault edited the proceedings of a conference on reclassification held at the Center of Adult Education, University of Maryland.[6] This includes valuable papers on the relationship between subject headings and classification, UDC as a candidate for reclassification, planning and personnel for reclassification to LC, workflow in reclassification, and the cost of reclassification.

The remainder of this chapter consists of case studies of reclassification in five British libraries.

University of Liverpool

The reclassification of Liverpool University's Harold Cohen Library from a home-made scheme to LC began in 1971, originally with one librarian tackling the German section and later with a team devoting virtually the whole of its time to the exercise. By 1973 this team consisted of an assistant librarian, two senior library assistants, three library assistants and two part-time processors. Only one of the team was normally employed in the cataloguing department, the others being seconded from public service departments.

The team tried to cover the largest classes such as History and English literature first, since these were also considered to be the most important from the point of view of the curriculum. Linked with this aim, however, was the very practical need to reduce the number of times books needed to be moved from shelf to shelf by reclassifying certain groups in order to make room on the shelf or to fill up empty shelves.

185

Generally the team of reclassifiers worked as three sub-groups on a subject basis. The assistant librarian and the two senior library assistants did the reclassification and helped with amendments in the catalogue; the library assistants (one attached to each of the three seniors) amended the catalogue entries by rubbing out the old pencilled class numbers and writing in new ones; and the processors relettered the books.

Use was made of the *National union catalog* when assigning new class numbers, though it was not followed slavishly. Indeed it could not be in view of the factual errors it was found to contain, such as mistakes in the birthplaces of some Latin American authors causing them to be classified incorrectly.

The target for reclassification was two hundred volumes per day, and this would normally have been achieved when the team was working at full strength but for various obstacles, most notably the introduction of the ALS (Automated Library System) charging system, which meant that the processors had to prepare books for ALS as well as relettering reclassified books.

After five years (in summer 1976), 118,443 volumes had been reclassified, representing about half the items needing reclassification. At that stage it was decided to dissolve the reclassification team and leave the faculty sub-librarians to organise their own reclassification.

In order to introduce the staff to the new system, five seminars were held in September 1974. These covered the overall outline of LC, the basic reasoning behind the notational structure and an explanation of the classification numbers chosen for a number of examples. The seminars concluded with the participants doing some practical classification on their own.

City of London Polytechnic

When the City of London Polytechnic was formed in 1970, the libraries of the constituent colleges were classified by a number of schemes including various editions of Dewey, the Universal Decimal Classification, Bliss's Bibliographic Classification and some home-made schemes. It was obviously desirable to use one scheme and the eighteenth edition of Dewey was chosen in order to allow effective use of MARC cataloguing services.

Reclassification began with the Business Studies Library, which had previously used BC, in May 1974. A team of three cataloguers, working solely on reclassification, completed the operation of reclassifying some 32,000 volumes in July 1976.

The procedure adopted was to work systematically through BC class by class, match the books with the catalogue cards, and make the necessary amendments. It was a definite policy only to reclassify with the book in hand and never from the catalogue entries alone.

Initially a computer printout was obtained from the British Library Bibliographic Services Division of all books appearing in the British National Bibliography between 1971 and 1973. This printout, which included the DC18 class number and the ISBN, enabled the work to proceed very quickly. When MARC records for the period 1950-1971 became available from BLBSD, it became possible to convert all material appearing in BNB to machine readable form.

A minor problem with the reclassification was that there was not always a direct match between BC and DC; for example, most books on management appear in class 650 of DC but in BC they may be in class K or class T, meaning that for a period books on management were classified in two places. In spite of this, reaction of both users and staff was favourable, DC being preferred to BC.

Reclassification of the other library sites commenced immediately after the completion of the reclassification of the Business Studies Library and is still (July 1977) in progress.

Bedford College (University of London)

The reclassification of Bedford College library from a home-made scheme to DC18 commenced in 1971 and is still in progress. While accepting that reclassification must not be undertaken lightly since it must inevitably cause some disruption over a period of years and place a considerable strain on library staff resources and on the forbearance of users, the librarian reported to his committee in 1969 that a) the existing situation was unsatisfactory and constituted a hindrance to intelligent and effective use of the library, and b) positive benefits would accrue from a programme of reclassification by a more widely accepted scheme.

The home-made scheme was based on departmental needs, and the process of reclassification was to take each department in turn and reclassify the collection by DC. In order to cause as little annoyance to readers as possible, material not on the shelves was not stopped in the issue and no staff or students were asked to return books simply so that they could be reclassified.

The reclassification programme was linked with recataloguing, using AACR and providing, for the first time, a classified catalogue and subject index. Thus the operation provided even greater benefits than the use of a more effective classification scheme.

Material in storage was not reclassified, nor is it likely to be reclassified in the future. This means that such material is excluded from the classified catalogue, but as it was removed to storage because it was little used this is not a major disadvantage. Another section of the library which will not be reclassified is the special collection of Dutch language and literature.

There was originally a team of two cataloguers concentrating entirely on reclassification, but now the cataloguing staff undertake reclassification in conjunction with the cataloguing and classification of new items.

Tavistock Joint Library

Reclassification of the Tavistock Joint Library was urgently needed in 1975 because a) there was no subject catalogue for the 10,000 books classified by the Bliss Bibliographic Classification and b) the 5,000 pamphlets containing some valuable information, were not classified at all.

Reclassification commenced in January 1976. The original plan was to classify reading room books in the first year, stack books in the second year and pamphlets in the third year, but this was modified partly because of delays in receiving the draft schedules of the revised BC. The order of reclassification must obviously be geared to the order in which the draft schedules are received. By October 1976 most books and pamphlets on Education (class J), Social welfare (Q), Philosophy (A), Statistics (AY) and Law (S) had been reclassified, as well as reading-room books on psychiatry. Recataloguing, including the provision of a classified catalogue and subject index entries, takes place at the same time as reclassification.

Until reclassification is completed there will obviously be two sequences of books, the reclassified items following those awaiting reclassification. A very practical point is the use of a different kind of lettering (using an electric stylus) for reclassified items so that it is immediately obvious which books have been reclassified and which have not.

Although a part-time classifier was appointed to take charge of the reclassification project, it is a deliberate policy of the librarian that all members of the staff are involved so that they become familiar with the scheme.

It is hoped and believed that the result of the reclassification exercise will be a more effectively organized library, allowing much more systematic handling of enquiries. The project has far wider implications than this, however, as the publication of the library's classified catalogue—a condition of the British Library's grant for reclassification —will provide an important subject bibliography.

The British Library (Science Reference Library)

The Science Reference Library (then the National Reference Library of Science and Invention) began reclassifying in 1964 from the classification scheme originally evolved by E Wyndham Hulme in the 1910s for the Patent Office Library (as it then was) to a new home-made scheme. The intellectual task of reclassifying over 50,000 books and periodicals from the Patent Office Library collection took several years. The scientific staff took it in turns to form a team to reclass the collection and to class the new acquisitions for Holborn. The procedure was as follows: 1 multiple Xerox copies were made of the 100,000 cards in the author catalogue; 2 these were rearranged in accession number order, thus bringing together all added author entries; 3 books for reclassification were removed from the shelves when required, a note to this effect being left until they were returned to their position on the shelves; 4 the books were reclassified on to a second accession sheet; 5 the books and cards were rubber stamped with the new class number and the cards sent for filing into multiple catalogues ready for use when the literature could be rearranged into the new order.

A reclassification/recataloguing routing sheet, used when changes become necessary within the SRL scheme and designed to ensure that all records are altered, is reproduced as figure twenty-two.

References
1 Baker Library, Harvard University Graduate School of Business Administration *A classification of business literature* 2nd ed, Hamden (Conn), Shoe String Press, 1960.
2 Personal communication from Lorna M Daniells.
3 Johnson, Edward R 'Applying "management by objectives" to the university library' *College and research libraries* 34(6) November 1973, 436-439.
4 Schriefer, Kent and Atkins, Gregg 'Reclassification at Berkeley' *Law library journal* 67(1) February 1974, 48-59.
5 Wassom, Earl E, Custead, Patricia W and Chen, Simon P 'On-line cataloging and circulation at Western Kentucky University: an approach to automated instructional resources management' *LARC report* (Library Automation Research and Consulting Association) 6(1) January 1973, 78p. *See also* Chen, Simon P J 'Automated cataloging and reclassification by ATS' *Special libraries* 64(4) April 1973, 193-197.
6 Perreault, J M (ed) *Reclassification: rationale and problems* College Park (Maryland), University of Maryland School of Library and Information Services, 1968.

(NOT for change or close of title, or disposal)

A. ORIGINATOR:

1. SRL   Location   (   )   -   (   )   Accession/
   Holborn POL "   Control no. S
   Bloomsbury POL "   Author &/or brief title:

2. Reason for alteration:

   a. Holdings change
   b. Schedule revision
   c. Location suspect 950 *
   d. Other class suspect 97 *
   e. 950/9, 958, 959 suspect *
       * enter class in C.2.b.

3. Other notes, if needed   **Initials & date**

                                     Originator   ...

B. SUPPORT (room 21) / PREPROCESSING:
     Input/accession sheets and volumes attached
     (with all analyticals if A.2.c. ticked)   ...   .

C. SUBJECT DESK: 1. Classing checked (all affected vols present)   ..

2.a. Fields	950 & 970		97 /	97 /	97 /
b. Original	( )	- ( )			
c. Change to:	( )	- ( )			

3. No changes? If so: Sections D, G, H, J, deleted   ...   .

4. Index entries checked: green forms SRL/83 attached   ...   .

5. Changes authorised, and subject/location records corrected   ..

D. SUPPORT: IF location altered:
                1. New unique no. (if necessary) allotted   ...   ..
                2. SRL 33 sent to Roneodex ...   .
                3. New location at G and in volumes(s)   ..   ..
                4. Check subject headings, if necessary   ...   ..
                5. Correct Om records, if any   ...   .

E. CATALOGUING: No change needed, & D deleted -- destroy this form.
     Changes needed: 1. Amended entries prepared
                    2. If location unchanged, return vol. to shelf
                    3. Accession sheet for withdrawal of entries   ..

or
F. CATALOGUING Section C.O.: 1. Cards altered by hand   ...   .
                            2. Accession sheet for filing   ...   ..

G. LABELLERS: All volumes relabelled as   ..

H. BOOK SERVICES:

1. Any boxes for this title relabelled as at G: vols etc reshelved
2. OLD location checked: 'new class' record left, and any parts
     there relabelled and reshelved at new location   ...   ..

J. ACQUISITIONS: Blue transfer slip, if any, amended. **Destroy this form.**

Figure 22: Reclassification/recataloguing routing sheet,
The British Library (Science Reference Library)

CLASSIFICATION OF TEN TITLES BY THE FIVE MAJOR
GENERAL SCHEMES IN SOME OF THE LIBRARIES VISITED

IN THIS APPENDIX I have listed ten well-known books with their class numbers in the five major general schemes as used in some of the libraries I visited. I was asked by one librarian why I did not also check the classification of some audio-visual materials in these libraries, and the obvious answer is that most libraries have very small collections of such materials so that it would have been difficult to choose suitable titles. I see no reason, however, why such materials should not be classified in exactly the same way as books, and this—as indicated in the foregoing chapters—is often the case.

The age of discontinuity (Drucker)
BC	(University of Lancaster)	KDN
CC	(Metal Box Limited)	X
DC	(Bedford College)	330.9
	(The City University)	301.24
	(University of Bradford)	301.23
LC	(Department of the Environment)	HC59
	(Edinburgh City Libraries)	HC54
UDC	(British Institute of Management)	338.5/.9
	(ICI Fibres)	33
	(University of Bath)	330

The ascent of man (Bronowski)
BC	(University of Lancaster)	AK3
CC		Y:1?
DC	(The City University)	301.243
LC	(Department of the Environment)	HM101
	(Edinburgh City Libraries)	Q125
UDC	(University of Bradford)	5

The British union catalogue of periodicals
BC	(University of Lancaster)	2J61ea
CC	(Metal Box Limited)	a46,94.2
DC	(The City University; University of Bradford)	016.05

LC	(Department of the Environment)	Z6941
	(Edinburgh City Libraries)	Z6945
UDC	(British Institute of Management; ICI Fibres)	016:05
	(University of Bath)	016.050

Encyclopaedia Britannica
BC	(University of Lancaster)	1
CC	(Metal Box Limited)	k
DC	(Bedford College; The City University; University of Bradford)	032
LC	(Department of the Environment; Edinburgh City Libraries)	AE5
UDC	(British Institute of Management)	03
	(ICI Fibres)	(03)
	(University of Bath)	030.1

Facts from figures (Moroney)
BC	(Department of Health and Social Security; University of Lancaster)	AY
CC	(Metal Box Limited)	B28
DC	(Bedford College)	518.3
	(The City University)	519.5024
LC	(Department of the Environment; Edinburgh City Libraries)	HA29
UDC	(British Institute of Management)	311
	(ICI Fibres; University of Bradford)	519.2
	(University of Bath)	519.01

Handbook of chemistry and physics
BC	(Department of Health and Social Security)	C1
CC	(Metal Box Limited)	A1
DC	(Bedford College)	540.0212
	(The City University)	530.8
LC	(Department of the Environment)	QD4
	(Edinburgh City Libraries)	QD65
UDC	(ICI Fibres)	(03)5

The practice of management (Drucker)
BC	(Department of Health and Social Security)	TJH
	(University of Lancaster)	TDG
CC	(Metal Box Limited)	X:8
DC	(Bedford College)	338.753
	(The City University)	658
LC	(Department of the Environment)	HF5546
	(Edinburgh City Libraries)	T58

UDC (British Institute of Management; ICI Fibres;   658
      University of Bath; University of Bradford)

Science for the citizen (Hogben)
BC	(University of Lancaster)	AK
CC	(Metal Box Limited)	A
DC	(The City University)	500
LC	(Edinburgh City Libraries)	Q162
UDC	(University of Bradford)	5

Scientific research in British universities and colleges
BC	(University of Lancaster)	1AK6
CC	(Metal Box Limited)	A:2y5:(T4:2)
DC	(Bedford College)	507.2042
	(The City University)	001.43
LC	(Department of the Environment)	Q181
	(Edinburgh City Libraries)	Q180
UDC	(British Institute of Management: vol 3 only)	
		058:3;001.5:378(41-4)
	(ICI Fibres)	5
	(University of Bath)	500.001(41)

Whitaker's almanack
BC	(Department of Health and Social Security)	1
	(University of Lancaster)	11
CC	(Metal Box Limited)	n.1
DC	(Bedford College)	300.25
	(The City University)	000
	(University of Bradford)	930
LC	(Department of the Environment)	AY752
	(Edinburgh City Libraries)	AY754
UDC	(British Institute of Management)	059
	(ICI Fibres)	(03)
	(University of Bath)	058

GLOSSARY

Alternative headings: a system of cataloguing whereby all entries are regarded as of equal status rather than one being designated 'main entry' and the others 'added entries'

Analytico-synthetic classification: a classification scheme which lists basic concepts and not compound subjects. The classifier specifies compound subjects by synthesising (building up) the notations for the appropriate concepts

Distributed relatives: aspects of the same subject which are separated by a classification scheme; for example, the economic aspects of automation may be classified in economics and the technical aspects in engineering, so automation is a 'distributed relative'.

Enumerative classification: a classification scheme which attempts to list all possible subjects, simple and compound. The Library of Congress scheme is the outstanding example

Facet analysis: the analysis of compound subjects into their basic concepts, each of which is grouped in an appropraite facet according to common characteristics or qualities

Faceted classification: see *Analytico-synthetic classification* and *Facet analysis*

Flexibility: the provision by a classification scheme of alternative treatments and/or locations for a subject

Hierarchical notation: a notation which attempts to reflect the hierarchy of the classification scheme, often by adding a digit for each subordinate subject. Also called expressive notation and structural notation

Hospitality: the ability of a notation to specify new terms added to a classification scheme

Mnemonics: memory aids in a classification scheme, normally by using the same notation to represent identical or similar concepts wherever they occur (systematic mnemonics). Some schemes use the initial letter of a term as the notation for that term (literal mnemonics), an example being C to represent Chemistry in the Bibliographic Classification

Non-hierarchical notation: a notation which simply indicates the order of a classification scheme without attempting to show hierarchical relationships

Notation: symbols used to represent the terms of a classification scheme

On-line system: a system in which there is direct communication with the central processing unit of a computer, allowing an operator to 'converse' directly with the computer and receive an almost immediate response to a message or instruction

Phase relationships: relationships between subjects from two different areas of a classification scheme, eg the influence of science on religion or mathematics for engineers

Post-co-ordinate indexing: a system of indexing in which a compound subject is analysed into its basic concepts by the indexer but these concepts are not combined until the search stage. Also frequently called co-ordinate indexing

Pre-co-ordinate indexing: a system of indexing in which a compound subject is analysed into its basic elements by the indexer, who then combines these elements in a predetermined order. Examples are entries in conventional classified and alphabetical subject catalogues

Retroactive notation: a system in which later sequences of notation in a faceted classification may be qualified by the earlier sequences, so that the appearance of an earlier symbol shows a change of facet

Systematic mnemonics: see *Mnemonics*

BASIC READING LIST

THE FOLLOWING BOOKS are cited on a number of occasions throughout this work. Bibliographical details given here have not been repeated with each citation.

Foskett, A C *The subject approach to information* 3rd ed. London, Bingley; Hamden (Conn), Linnet, 1977. (Cited as: Foskett)

Maltby, Arthur (ed) *Clasification in the 1970s: a second look* Revised ed. London, Bingley; Hamden (Conn), Linnet, 1976. (Cited as: Maltby)

Maltby, Arthur *Sayers' manual of classification for librarians* 5th ed. London, Deutsch, 1975. (Cited as Maltby/Sayers)

INDEX

THE INDEX is arranged alphabetically letter-by-letter, spaces and punctuation between words being ignored. Thus CRG follows Crestadoro and Environment Canada follows Environmental.

Classification schemes are entered under their titles; in the case of *Bliss Bibliographical Classification* and *Dewey Decimal Classification* the original authors' surnames are regarded as integral parts of the title. Universities and other corporate bodies are entered directly under their names, in accordance with *Anglo-American cataloguing rules 1967*, though the AACR heading 'Great Britain' has been omitted from entries for British government departments. In all cases cross-references are made from alternative forms of name or, if the need for economy allows it, additional entries are made.

A page reference followed by b indicates a bibliographical reference.

Abbreviations and acronyms used in the index are explained on pages 11-12.

Austin, Derek 168b
Australian national bibliography 154
Automated Library System 186

Baker Library, Harvard University Graduate School of Business Administration 182, 183, 189b
Bakewell, K G B 142b, 169b
Ball, Douglas 135, 142b
Barnard, C C, *Classification for medical libraries* 77
Barnholdt, B 52b
Batty, C David 34, 36b, 100b
Batty, Ellen L 168b
BCM Classification 116-9, 141b
Bedford College (University of London)
    chain indexing 20
    DC 19-22, 191-3
    reclassification 187-8
Beecham Products 137
Belton, M 169b
Benbow, J A 53b
Beswick, Norman 29, 36b, 170, 171, 180b
Bias phase
    CC 95
    LEC 127
    SRL classification 113
Bibliographical Retrieval Service 177
Bibliographic Classification see Bliss Bibliographic Classification
Bibliographies
    classification: Lagos University (LC) 72
Bibliothèque Nationale 34
Biography
    classification: DC 14, 16; Hazel Grove High School (DC) 32
Birds
    classification: SRL 111, 113-4

Birmingham Libraries Co-operative Mechanization Project. Music and Sound Recordings Subgroup 118
Birmingham Public Libraries, BCM at 117-8
Birmingham School of Music, BCM at 117-8
Blagden, John F 176, 180b
BLAISE 156
BLCMP Music and Sound Recordings Subgroup 118
Bliss Bibliographic Classification 26, 76-93
    advantages 82
    chain indexing problems 144
    DHSS 77-81, 192-3
    future 91-2
    literal mnemonics 195
    NFER 81-2
    problems 86, 90, 91
    reclassification from 186-7
    reclassification to 188
    revised edition 76; 81, 89-92
    Tavistock Joint Library 89-91
    University of Lancaster 82-6, 191-3
    Zoological Society of London 86-9
Bliss Classification Association 76, 91
Bliss Classification bulletin 76
Bliss, H E 76, 113
Bloom, Janet 13, 36b, 55, 74b
BNB *see British national bibliography*
Book indexing, importance of 132
Boreal Institute of Northern Studies 51
Boston University 149
Bradford University *see* University of Bradford
British catalogue of music classification 116-9, 141b

202

South Africa 35
South Trafford College of
  Further Education 24, 26
United States 13-15, 56
University of Bradford 16-19,
  191-3
use of 04 14
vs Cheltenham Classification,
  for schools 102-3
Dialog Information Retrieval
  Service 177, 179
Dictionary catalogues 148-51
Difference phase
  CC 95
  LEC 127
Distributed relatives
  DC 20, 27, 29, 31, 33
  definition 194
Divided catalogues 148-9, 150-1
Dixon, Geoffrey 142b
Documentation Research and
  Training Centre, Bangalore 100
Downing, Joel C 13, 34, 35b,
  36b

Eare, Anthony J 77, 92b
Eaves, D 75b, 92b
Economics
  classification: Croham
    Hurst School (Cheltenham
    Classification) 103; Univer-
    sity of Bath (UDC) 43
Edinburgh City Libraries
  alphabetical subject index
    147-8
  LC 61-4, 191-3
  LCSH 149
Edinburgh University Central
  Medical Library 107
Edney, Patience 130, 142b
Education
  classification: Croham Hurst
    School (Cheltenham

Education (cont'd)
    Classification) 104; Hazel
    Grove High School (DC) 32;
    LEC 123, 126-33; NFER (BC)
    81-2; University of Bath (UDC)
    43; University of Lancaster
    (BC) 85
Educational Resources Information
  Center 177, 180b
Einstein (Albert) School of
  Medicine 107
EJC thesaurus 121, 122, 142b
Elliott, Pirkka 142b
Elrod, J McRee 73b
Energy
    classification: Departments of
      the Environment and Trans-
      port (LC) 68
Energy facet (CC) 94-5
Engineering
    classification: *Thesaurofacet*
      119-23
Engineering index 152
Engineers' Joint Council *Thesaurus
  of engineering and scientific
  terms* 121, 122, 142b
English Electric Company *see
  Thesaurofacet*
English language
    classification: University of
      Lancaster (BC) 83
English literature
    classification: Bedford
      College (DC) 21; University
      of Bradford (DC) 18;
      University of Lancaster (BC)
      83-5
Enumerative Classification,
  definition 194
Environmental health
    classification: Departments of
      the Environment and Trans-
      port (LC) 67

203

Environmental problems
classification: South Trafford
College of Further Education (DC) 24
Environment Canada 51
Enyingi, Peter 150, 168b
ERIC 177, 180b
EUDISED thesaurus 133, 142b
European Economic Community
classification: City University
(DC) 24; Edinburgh City
Libraries (LC) 64
Exeter Regional Resources
Centre 91
Expansive Classification 9-10
Expressive notation *see*
Hierarchical notation

Facet analysis
definition 194
in alphabetical subject
headings 152-9
in ANBAR Decimal
Classification 138-9
in CC 94-100
in DC, as used at University
of Bradford 18-19
in LCBS 136
in UDC, an advantage 51
Fairview Hospital, Minneapolis
178
False drops 171
Feature cards 170-6
Fegan, E S, *Cheltenham
Classification* 26, 101-6, 141b
Feng, Cyril C H 180b
Fish, R 88
Flexibility
BC 82, 91
definition 194
UDC 51
Fluid mechanics
classification: City

University (DC) 23; SRL
112, 114-5
Flury, William R 169b
Foci (CC) 94
Foreman, Gertrude 180b
Foskett, A C 37b, 52, 54b,
75b, 92b, 100b, 196b
Foskett, D J and Joy, *London
Education Classification* 123,
126-33, 142b
Freeman, R R 50, 52b, 53b
French language
classification: University of
Bath (UDC) 39-41
French literature
classification: Edinburgh
City Libraries (LC) 62
Friedman, Joan 9
Friis-Hansen, J B 35, 36b, 37b

Gagne, Frank X 161
GEC Power Engineering 121
Geographical subdivision
Departments of the
Environment and Transport
(LC) 68
University of Liverpool (LC)
58-9
Wigan Reference Library (LC)
70-1
Geography
classification: Abridged BC
77; Cheltenham Classifica-
tion 102; Croham Hurst
School (Cheltenham
Classification) 104; DC 20,
33; Parliament Hill School
(DC) 31; UDC 39
German literature
classification: University of
Bath (UDC) 42
Gomersall, Alan 141b; *see also
Thesaurofacet*

206

Modifications to classification
schemes, dangers of 72
Mowery, Robert L 10, 56, 74b
Music
  classification: BCM 116-9;
    Edinburgh City Libraries
    (LC) 62; University of
    Lancaster (BC) 85

National Federation of Abstract-
  ing and Indexing Services 50
National Foundation for
  Educational Research in
  England and Wales
    BC 81-2
    *Register of educational
    research in the United
    Kingdom* 132-3
National insurance
  classification: DHSS (BC)
  79-80
National Library of Medicine
  classification 106-10, 141b,
  177-9
  Medical subject headings
  150-1
National Library of Scotland,
  BCM at 117
National Oceanographic Data
  Center 50
National Reference Library of
  Science and Invention *see*
  British Library (Science
  Reference Library)
National union catalog 56, 58,
  186
Natural Rubber Producers'
  Research Association 152
Needham, Angela 167, 169b
Beil, A G 127, 142b
NELINET 149
New England Library Network 149
New York Academy of
  Medicine 107

New York, State University of
  107
NLM *see* National Library of
  Medicine
Non-book materials
  City of London Polytechnic
    (DC) 24, 25
  City University (DC) 24
  Codsall High School (OCCI)
    170-3
  Edinburgh City Libraries 63-4
  Exeter Regional Resources
    Centre (BC) 91-2
  Hazel Grove High School
    (OCCI) 173-6
  ILEA Centre for Learning
    Resources (DC) 26-9
  Parliament Hill School (DC)
    31-2
  St Thomas the Apostle School,
    London (DC) 30
  Schools Council (LEC) 132
  South Trafford College of
    Further Education 26, 145-7
  University of Bath (UDC) 43
  University of Bradford (DC &
    UDC) 19
  University of Lancaster (BC)
    85, 86
  University of London
    Institute of Education (LEC)
    127-8
Non-hierarchical notation
  advantages 116, 137
  BC 144
  BCM 116
  definition 195
  disadvantages 57, 116, 144
  LC 57, 69
  LCBS (Manchester Business
    School adaptation) 137
North Carolina Science and
  Technology Research Center
  179

Recreation
  classification: Departments of
    the Environment and Trans-
    port (LC) 65-6
Reeves, Harold 118, 141b
*Register of educational research
  in the United Kingdom 1973-
  1976* 132-3
Religion
  classification: Edinburgh
    City Libraries (LC) 61-2
Resource centres
  classification: British Library
    (LA Library) (DC) 33
  OCCI in 170-6
  see also Non-book materials
Retroactive notation
  BC 81, 90
  BCM 116
  definition 195
Ribboning, SRL classification
  112-3
Richmond, Phyllis 57, 74b
Rigby, Malcolm 50, 52b
Roads
  classification: Departments
    of the Environment and
    Transport (LC) 66-7
Rockefeller University 107
Rotation of index entries
  BIM (UDC) 45-6
  Schools Council (LEC) 131
  University of London
    Institute of Education (LEC)
    128
  Royal Army Medical College
    107
Ruck, J 92b
Russell, M 52b

St George's Hospital, London 107
St Katherine's College,
  Liverpool 92

St Luke's College of Education,
  Exeter 92
St Thomas the Apostle School,
  Peckham, DC and chain
  indexing at 30
Sandison, A 110, 141b
Savage, E A 55, 61, 73b
Sayers, W C Berwick 37b,
  53b, 75b, 92b, 99, 100b, 196b
Scheerer, George 106, 141b
Schimmelpfeng, Richard H 74b
School libraries
  BC 76-7
  Cheltenham Classification
    101-6
  DC 29-33, 172
  OCCI 170-6
  see also Inner London
    Education Authority Central
    Library Resources Service
School Library Association 76
School resource centres *see* Non-
  book materials; Resource
  centres
Schools Council
  LEC 130-2
  Resource Centre project 29,
    170
Schriefer, Kent 184, 189b
Science
  classification: Cheltenham
    Classification 105;
    Croham Hurst School
    (Cheltenham Classification)
    104; SRL 110-5
Science Reference Library *see*
  British Library (Science
  Reference Library)
Scope notes
  CRG 133
  LEC 123, 128, 130
  SRL 114-5
Scott Polar Research Institute 51

Secondary education
classification: Hazel Grove
High School (DC) 32
Selective dissemination of
information, with UDC 49
Selective listing in combination
161-3, 164-6, 167
Selwood, R 142b
Sharp, John R 161, 169b
Sheffield City Polytechnic,
PRECIS at 157, 159, 160
Shifrin, Malcolm 26, 29, 36b
SLIC indexing 161-3, 164-6,
167
Smith, J C 39
SMRE bibliography 159
Social biology
problem of classifying
with DC 26
Social Science Research
Council 138
Social security
classification: DHSS (BC)
79-80
Social services
classification: City University
(DC) 23; Croham Hurst
School (Cheltenham
Classification) 104
Social surveys
classification: Hazel Grove
High School (DC) 32
Social welfare
classification: University of
Bradford (DC) 18
Sociology
classification: Croham
Hurst School (Cheltenham
Classification) 103-4
Sophandorn, Kanchana 107,
141b
South Trafford College of
Further Education (continues)

South Trafford (cont'd)
alphabetical subject index
145-7
DC 24, 26
Space facet (CC) 95
Special classification schemes
101-43
Special libraries *see* Academic
libraries; Beecham Products;
British Institute of Management;
British Library (Library Associa-
tion Library); British Library
(Science Reference Library);
British Standards Institution
Technical Help for Exporters;
Bronswerk NV; Business Archives
Council; Civil Service Depart-
ment; Department of Health
and Social Security; Departments
of the Environment and Trans-
port; Environment Canada;
Fairview Hospital; GEC Power
Engineering; ICI Fibres;
Institute of Personnel Manage-
ment; Institute of Practitioners
in Work Study, Organization
and Methods; International
Nickel Company of Canada;
Irish Department of Education;
Law libraries; Mayo Clinic;
Metal Box Limited; Mitre
Corporation; National Founda-
tion for Educational Research;
Natural Rubber Producers'
Research Association; New York
Academy of Medicine; North
Carolina Science and Technology
Research Center; Northwestern
Hospital; Pfizer Inc; Poole
General Hospital; St George's
Hospital; Schools Council;
Tavistock Joint Library; Western
Australia Government Railways;

Special libraries (cont'd)
Zoological Society of
London
Spriggs, Susan 142b
SRC 51-2
SRL *see* British Library
(Science Reference Library)
Standard reference (roof)
code 51-2
State University of New York
107
Structural notation *see*
Hierarchical notation
Stuart-Jones, E A L 142b
Subject field reference code
51-2
Sweeney, Russell 36b, 74b
Sydney School of Public
Health and Tropical
Medicine 150
Synthesis
absence in LC a disadvantage
59-60
absence in SRL 114
BC 76, 78-83, 85, 88-91
BCM 116-9
LCBS 136-7
LEC 126-8
Thesaurofacet 120
see also Analytico-
synthetic classification
Systematic mnemonics,
definition 195
System Development Corpora-
tion 177, 179

Tagliacozzo, Renata 178, 180b
Tasmania, University of 73, 91
Tauber, M F 56, 74b, 170,
179b
Tavistock Joint Library
BC 89-91
reclassification 188
Taylor, Gerry M 74b

Technological University Library
of Denmark 49-50
Textile industries
classification: ICI Fibres (UDC)
48-9
Thesauri *see* ERIC; *EUDISED
thesaurus; London education
classification; Management
information retrieval; Thesaurofacet; Thesaurus of engineering
and scientific terms*
Thesaurofacet 119-23, 137, 141b
British Standards Institution
Technical Help for Exporters
122-3, 124-5
*Thesaurus of engineering and
scientific terms* 121, 122, 142b
Tidy, P 173
Time facet (CC) 95
Tool phase (LEC) 127
Top management abstracts 143b
Topography
classification: Edinburgh
City Libraries (LC) 63;
Wigan Reference Library (LC)
71
Tourism
classification: Departments of
the Environment and Trans-
port (LC) 65-6
Trade
classification: University of
Bath (UDC) 43
Traffic organization and control
classification: Departments
of the Environment and
Transport (LC) 66
Transport
classification: Departments
of the Environment and
Transport (LC) 66; Parlia-
ment Hill School (DC) 31
Transportation planning
classification: Departments

214